FROM
SAINTS
TO **WINNERS**

FROM
SAINTS
TO WINNERS

THE STORY OF
NORTHAMPTON SAINTS'
HISTORIC DOUBLE-WINNING SEASON

TOM VICKERS

First published by Pitch Publishing, 2017

Pitch Publishing
A2 Yeoman Gate
Yeoman Way
Worthing
Sussex
BN13 3QZ
www.pitchpublishing.co.uk
info@pitchpublishing.co.uk

A CIP catalogue record is available for this book
from the British Library.

ISBN 978-1-78531-320-2

Typesetting and origination by Pitch Publishing

Printed in the UK by TJ International, Cornwall

Contents

Foreword

IN professional sport you are always looking forward; the next passage of play, the next game, your next signing, the next campaign. It is also one of the biggest clichés to say that in sport you are judged primarily on your next result, not necessarily on the years that have gone before, so to rest on your laurels can be very dangerous, especially in a league as competitive as the Aviva Premiership.

However, when I was asked to write the foreword to this book, I took the opportunity to reflect on a season which will go down as one of the best, if not *the* best, in my career and in the careers of our coaches, players and staff at Franklin's Gardens.

It was a season that was full of highs and yet also some significant setbacks, which could well have derailed the campaign. There was a large home loss to Leinster in the Heineken Cup, another home loss to Leicester in the Aviva Premiership and a disappointing defeat to Exeter at Sandy Park in the LV= Cup Final, the first of three finals the team would reach in the year.

Most memorable for me was how the squad responded to these setbacks. The Leinster game at the Gardens was crushing. Nothing went right and the defeat was devastating for all. The players had less than a week to absorb the shock, pick themselves up and face the same team on their home ground. In spite of a back line full of injuries, players playing out of position and facing a confident, quality side, the boys took to the field determined to win.

This was accomplished in front of more than 40,000 people, the vast majority of whom were stunned into silence. It wasn't easy. Leinster played well and although we went ahead early in the game, we spent a great deal of time defending, not least in the final minutes when they were pressing for what would have been the match-winning try. But we held out, turned the ball over, and Jamie Elliott went the length of the pitch for a try of our own. This was a fantastic way to end what had been a week of hard work and determination. It showed what we were about as a team.

Then in March we had three poor losses on consecutive weekends, including the LV= Cup Final and away to Sale in the Aviva Premiership. Having qualified for the quarter-final of the Amlin Challenge Cup we were then faced with a short turnaround for the Thursday night game back at Sale. With many of the squad having played in the Six Nations Championship, we made a large number of changes to the starting line-up.

But, just as our squad players had stepped up during the Six Nations Championship and autumn internationals with wins that helped us achieve a top two finish and the home Aviva Premiership semi-final, they also returned home from the AJ Bell Stadium with a comfortable win which gave us a home semi-final against Harlequins. We would not have won the Challenge Cup without those performances, which is why Tom Wood and myself took time to pay tribute to all those players after the final win over Bath in Cardiff.

Those two weeks in May were some of the most emotional in my time in rugby. We had the Aviva Premiership semi-final home win over Leicester, a game that we won with a last-minute try that took the roof off Franklin's Gardens. It was far and away the best atmosphere I've experienced at our stadium, and my reaction – indeed the reaction of all of us – showed the release of tension and emotion, which had come from beating our local rivals. In the past, against Leicester, we have had some narrow defeats in big games, not least the Aviva Premiership Final a year before. We knew that we were fitter than Leicester, and that if we kept playing we could win the game, regardless of how many players were on the pitch, and we did exactly that.

Then came Cardiff, and with the Aviva Premiership Final still to come, the players could perhaps have kept something back for Twickenham. But everyone wanted to play, everyone was determined to win silverware, and having gone behind in the first half, we kept our heads, stuck to our game plan, and eventually came home with a comfortable win.

And of course there was the Aviva Premiership Final itself. Saracens and ourselves had been involved in European finals the weekend before, but both teams emptied their tanks completely in a game that swung from one side to the other and eventually became the first final to go into extra-time. Trailing by three points going into the last minute, we were attacking deep in their 22, and I can admit now, that I wanted Stephen Myler to take the drop goal because we would have won on tries scored. If a try decision goes to the TMO it is in the lap of the gods, especially at the bottom of a ruck.

We've got a photo in the Crooked Hooker at Franklin's Gardens, taken from the stands, showing Alex Waller had got the ball on the line. With TV angles not having the same view, it was a hairline decision that thankfully the match officials got correct!

The following day we had the open top-bus parade. Turning into Northampton's town centre to see 30,000 supporters was fantastic. On a personal level I was even more delighted that

Keith Barwell was able to join us on the bus and to see first-hand the impact of our success on the rest of the town. The Saints would not be where they are without Keith and it was right that he was there with the players and staff.

Cup finals and wins are built on months of hard work done away from the public eye and in this I would like to pay tribute to all the support staff at Franklin's Gardens. These include our medical, performance and coaching teams plus our administrators, sales, marketing and community teams who generate the income which allows us to invest in the playing side. It was a full staff effort and something of which we can all be proud.

In the spring we had a trip to La Santa in Lanzarote, which proved an invaluable opportunity for the players to recharge and bond before going into the crucial final weeks of the season. We then posted a record score against Wasps, which set the momentum for the knock-out wins which followed.

Winning was certainly contagious during the year and while the big trophies came home in May, the success began earlier than that. The Wanderers reached the final of the Aviva A League in the December, losing only to a strong Bath team, and the Under-18s won the Premiership Rugby Academies' League in the February, beating a strong, in-form Exeter side, in the final at Allianz Park.

These achievements were inspiring for the whole squad and gave all the players involved the confidence to know that they could contribute and be an important part of the wider effort.

Finally, it is only right to pay tribute to all of our supporters who believed in and followed the team during the campaign. We had nine months of games, week in and week out. Every time we played we were greeted by a sea of black, green and gold, in mighty fine chorus.

Twickenham was of course the highlight of this, with more than half the stadium wearing our colours. Following a team across the country and in Europe requires commitment, both in terms of time and money. The large groups of Saints supporters everywhere we went showed the passion and feeling they have for their club.

We hoped and indeed believed that 2013/14 would be the start of many Premiership-winning seasons to come for Northampton Saints. Yet the first time is always the most special, and deserves to be remembered with a smile on all of our faces.

Jim Mallinder
Director of rugby, Northampton Saints

Introduction

'JP, you may award the try.' Those six words signalled an historic moment in the history of Northampton Saints as Alex Waller was awarded a score that brought the club's first Premiership title.

Referee JP Doyle, having received confirmation from Television Match Official (TMO), Graham Hughes, that prop Waller had got the ball down, raised his left arm and put his whistle to his lips. The shrill sound sparked jubilation on the pitch and in the stands as the army of Saints fans who had travelled to Twickenham for the second year in succession saw their side finally get over the line.

Memories of agonising semi-final defeats and the previous year's final loss at the hands of bitter rivals Leicester Tigers were banished as hooker Ross McMillan hoisted a battered and bruised Waller into the south-west London sky.

Director of rugby Jim Mallinder and attack coach Alex King shared a warm embrace, with relief and immense satisfaction sinking in at the end of the most memorable of seasons.

The supporters, decked out in the green, black and gold of one of the country's most famous clubs, copied Mallinder and King, clutching each other in sheer disbelief and palpable adulation. The waiting was over.

Northampton Saints were champions of England.

Summer of 2013

THE summer of 2013 was spent rebuilding, on and off the pitch, mentally and physically. Saints had entered the off-season on the back of a Premiership Final defeat to bitter local rivals, Leicester Tigers.

During what was a tempestuous Twickenham encounter, captain Hartley had been red-carded for verbally abusing referee Wayne Barnes, who had alleged that the hooker had called him a 'f****** cheat' in awarding Leicester a penalty just before half-time.

It was to be the beginning of the end for Saints' chances of lifting the silverware as, despite a hugely spirited second-half showing, they eventually fell on their sword, losing 37-17.

Hartley was later handed an 11-week ban, which cost him his place on the Lions' tour of Australia, giving Ireland's Rory Best a late chance to grab a seat on the plane to Hong Kong.

Hartley would not be eligible to play again until 1 September, but more pressing was the need to get away from it all. To refresh his mind and banish the immense disappointment of being absent from a tour that he could almost touch. He had even been sent the official team clothing.

The club captain's summer was almost a microcosm of the club's as a whole as Saints were forced to deal with that crushing Twickenham disappointment and use it as fuel for a fresh challenge the year after. They had carried themselves under the 'Why not us?' banner during a campaign that had seen them overcome mid-season struggles to eventually shock Saracens in a stunning semi-final at Allianz Park and book the trip to Twickenham.

But rather than remaining plucky underdogs, they harboured a desire to be so much more when it all began again in September. They didn't want to use criticism as their main motivation, as they had on the road to their first Premiership Final.

Thankfully for the club's fans, there was solace to be found in the players that had been recruited ahead of the new season. World-class Wales wing George North and England loosehead prop Alex Corbisiero, both of whom were to play key roles in the Lions' 2-1 series win Down Under, were among the men heading to Franklin's Gardens that summer.

They were to be joined by Samoan scrum half Kahn Fotuali'i, who whetted the appetite of the Northampton faithful with a try for the Barbarians against the Lions in Hong Kong in June. He arrived with a reputation for being one of, if not *the* best number nine, in the world and there was widespread excitement that his signature had been secured.

To add to the men who would put the plans into action on the pitch, Saints also recruited a man some felt would be the best signing of the lot. King, an attack coach of real repute, was acquired from Clermont Auvergne, filling the void left by club legend Paul Grayson, who had left the Gardens in the November of that turbulent 2012/13 season.

Saints had been seeking to freshen things up and they felt moving Grayson on would open the door to new ideas. In walked King, a former Wasps and England fly half, who had arrived in France as a player, but later moved into a coaching role at Clermont, cutting his teeth under the tuition of men such as Vern Cotter and Joe Schmidt.

King was a bright young thing among the continent's coaching fraternity and it was felt he could be the man who could take Northampton to the next level – to get the heavy artillery they were assembling to really fire, at home and abroad.

His arrival was to have the desired effect of shaking things up for a club desperate to seize its chance after going so close the season before.

'They were obviously very strong because they had got to the final the season before and they came close to winning that final,' King says, as he looks back on his arrival at the club.

'There wasn't a huge amount of change – it was just about getting a balance to the work between the backs and the forwards and I tried to make sure one unit wasn't doing the bulk of the work.

'We wanted to share the workload, so that was the main thing, and we had to make sure we had some leadership in the backs. We had Stephen Myler and Lee Dickson, with Dylan Hartley and Tom Wood in the forwards, so we did have those leaders across the board.'

Those players, along with new arrivals like North and Fotuali'i, clearly tempted King to swap France for England.

'I already knew what a great squad it was, so to add the likes of George and Kahn to it, I knew we would be in a good position,' King says. 'It puts fear into the opposition.

'I knew Jim Mallinder, Dorian West and Alan Dickens for a while before moving to Northampton and I knew what a well-run club it was. It was traditional, with great fans, a great stadium, a great history and an even better future.

'I knew I would be very lucky to be involved and I wanted to help them compete.'

King would certainly do that and his arrival was part of one of the largest-scale set of close-season changes that the club had seen under Mallinder, the director of rugby, who had taken over in the summer of 2007. It was a revolving door at the Gardens as though the likes of Corbisiero, Fotuali'i, North and Australian prop Salesi Ma'afu came in, stalwarts such as Soane Tonga'uiha and Brian Mujati moved on.

Props Tonga'uiha and Mujati, so crucial to helping Saints establish themselves as one of the best packs in Europe, especially during the run to the 2010/11 Heineken Cup Final, had opted to move to Racing Metro in France, cashing in on their talents during the latter years of their impressive careers.

It meant Saints would have to hope men such as Corbisiero and Ma'afu could shoulder the forward burden, while the likes of Academy graduate Alex Waller and his brother Ethan knew they would get the chance to really make their mark in the next few years.

As it turned out, they wouldn't have much to worry about.

However, while Saints were bidding fond farewells to established on-field figures, they were also saying a sad goodbye off it.

Leon Barwell, the chairman, lost his battle with cancer, passing away at the age of just 46 in the June of that year. The affable figurehead had clung on so bravely, showing his desperation to defy his wretched illness and watch Saints in the final at Twickenham.

Unfortunately his team could not deliver the win on that sun-soaked May day, but they were soon pledging to do it for him during the next campaign, with #ForLeon doing the rounds on social media site Twitter.

More than 900 people packed into All Saints Church in Northampton town centre for the funeral of the much-loved man, who had taken over the role as chairman from his father, Keith, and put so much into it.

Next is the tribute I wrote after hearing of his passing ...

Leon Barwell: a man of action, a man of the people, a true Saintsman.

That is how I will remember the former Northampton chairman, who sadly passed away aged just 46 on Friday morning.

Having met Leon on a number of occasions, it was clear to me that this was a man of the utmost sincerity.

He was a genuine character unbowed by the rigours of professional rugby and by the illness he endured for a long period of his reign at Franklin's Gardens.

During his 18 months as Saints chairman, Leon did not just sit back and rest on the good work done by his father, Keith, before him.

No, Leon was a man of action. He did a sterling job to ensure the club was competitive, on and off the pitch.

Saints continue to be stable financially, thanks to the good work of the Barwell family, allowing the team to consistently challenge for honours at the top of the game.

A tight ship has been run, but director of rugby Jim Mallinder has not been short of backing.

This summer, the likes of George North and Kahn Fotuali'i have arrived to bolster the squad. And what a squad it should be next season.

It is just an immense shame that Leon will not be at the Gardens next season to see his good work come to fruition.

But the sight of him at Twickenham on Grand Final day will live long in the memory.

Though it wasn't the result Saints wanted, the fact their chairman defied his illness to watch his final game at HQ was a huge achievement in itself.

But, typical of Leon, he did not just sit in the stands and watch on as events unfolded. At the game's conclusion, he made his way on to the pitch to console his players.

He put an arm around Dylan Hartley, when the skipper, who was sent off during the game, needed it most.

Leon was a man of the people.

And it's not just those working at the club he reached out to. His warmth extended to the supporters, too.

When some were questioning the club's approach midway through the season, with the team struggling, Leon stepped in.

He was the catalyst for events such as the fans' forum in February and April's open day. Both were a huge success, and both restored faith in the club and the professional game.

Leon expressed his desire to bring back the 'old-fashioned rugby club culture', with barriers between players and fans broken down. He did that.

For me, he was never anything but a pleasure to deal with. He was always on the end of the phone if questions needed to be asked. Some shy away from the media, fearing it as if it's an ogre about to beat down the door. But Leon didn't.

When whispers reached me about the possible signing of North – one of the biggest in the club's history – Leon was happy to give me an on-the-record reply.

He thought carefully about what he said, before giving me a story for which I will forever be grateful.

Even when I called him during a skiing holiday, he fielded the call and spoke kindly from on the slopes.

Put simply, his was an approach which should be a lesson to whoever takes over the role of chairperson at Northampton.

Leon's legacy lives on. He was a true Saintsman.

Tony Hewitt, a long-time friend of the Barwell family and a man involved with the Saints for 25 years, had taken over as acting chairman when Leon stepped down eight days before passing away, and Hewitt was to take on the role on a permanent basis in September.

However, Leon's legacy certainly did live on and the passion he felt for the club was to be carried by the players into the new campaign as they looked to make good their promise of doing it for him.

Pre-season

BY the time the pre-season encounters rolled round, Saints had sharpened their focus and many of their men had reason to be cheerful ahead of the return to the battlefield. While the seemingly unstoppable North and reinvigorated Corbisiero, who claimed he was 'in the best shape of his life', had celebrated a stunning Lions triumph in Australia, several other stars had been strutting their stuff for England.

With many of their key men with the Lions, Stuart Lancaster's Red Rose had travelled to South America for a two-Test tour of Argentina. There were plenty of Saints players present, with Ben Foden, Tom Wood, Courtney Lawes, Lee Dickson, Luther Burrell and Stephen Myler among those involved.

Burrell and Myler appeared for the England senior side for the first time in a game against a CONSUR XV in Montevideo as they warmed up for the clashes with the Pumas. England were to prevail 2-0 in the series as they showed they could do without their Lions players, and the suspended Hartley.

Not only that, but there was more reason for those of an English persuasion to celebrate during the summer, as the Under-20s, who had Saints duo Alex Day and Danny Hobbs-Awoyemi in their squad, won the Junior World Championships with a satisfying final victory over Wales in France. All in all, it was quite a summer for those of a Saints persuasion, and their club were to reap the rewards of their international springboard during a blemish-free pre-season campaign.

With the Premiership fixtures announced, Mallinder's men knew they would need to be in good shape come the start of the serious stuff, as they were handed a tough opening set of matches. The season was to start at home to Exeter Chiefs on 7 September, before testing trips to Harlequins and Gloucester.

With that in mind, there was a necessity for Saints to hit the ground running in pre-season and they would need to integrate their host of new signings quickly in a bid to ensure there was no sluggishness from the off.

The first chance to blow away the summer cobwebs came at Goldington Road in the middle of August, with Bedford Blues, a familiar pre-season opponent, lying in wait.

Prior to the match, fly half Myler had been waxing lyrical about new number nine Fotuali'i, going as far as to say that the Samoan would 'take us to that next level'.

Meanwhile, Mallinder was setting the spotlight on King, claiming the 38-year-old had added 'something different' to the Gardens mix and discussing the 'good ideas' he had brought with him across the Channel.

Those ringing endorsements from Myler and Mallinder proved to be more than just platitudes as the work of King and Fotuali'i instantly shone through against a Blues side who were, at times, bamboozled by Saints.

Fotuali'i was only on the field for the first 40 minutes, but during that time he showed signs of the stardust he would add to the Saints squad and he set up a try for South African No.8 GJ van Velze. Gareth Denman, a prop who had arrived from Rotherham, and new Kiwi lock Rob Verbakel were also able to get some game time as Saints overcame the concession of a first-half hat-trick to Blues full back Mark Atkinson to secure a 45-21 win.

The victory was earned thanks to 26 unanswered second-half points and it was entertaining fare for those who made the trip from Northampton on a warm Friday night.

Saints spent the rest of the weekend tackling a World Club Sevens tournament at Twickenham, with Tom Stephenson the stand-out performer in a format that has never exactly been Northampton's forte.

There wasn't to be much success on the hallowed turf, but the more important matter of 15-a-side combat soon returned, with two games to look forward to in as many days in the week that followed.

First up was a trip to Moseley's quaint Billesley Common ground, where a largely inexperienced Saints side shone in the sun, eventually earning a 38-32 success against the battle-hardened Championship outfit.

The following day saw Edinburgh head to the Gardens and the wait was finally over. North and Corbisiero made their Northampton bows in front of the excited Franklin's Gardens faithful, who saw their team claim a comfortable 24-6 triumph.

The anticipation was noticeable every time North got the ball, with fans desperate to see more of the heroics that lit up the Lions tour. The behemoth back had taken the Aussies to task, scoring tries and even carrying opposition full back Israel Folau on his shoulders in an almighty show of strength during the second Test in Melbourne.

However, he was more inclined to leave the Edinburgh players on the ground with a few of his trademark runs pushing the Scots to the floor as Saints stepped up their pre-season preparations with another win.

It was not North or fellow Lions star Corbisiero who stole the show though, as Saints stalwart Phil Dowson took the plaudits with a quick-fire second-half double. Burrell later credited his side's superior fitness for the success and they were certainly up and running as they got set for their final friendly, and the one which was likely to be the toughest of the lot.

Leinster were lying in wait at Dublin's archaic Donnybrook Stadium on the final Friday of August, but this was not your typical Leinster side. The hosts were without all of their Ireland and British & Irish Lions stars and instead called on a youthful crop of players.

In contrast, Saints were as strong as they could be as they knew there was just one more run-out remaining before it all began eight days later with the visit of Exeter. Ultimately, the men from Northampton were too strong, dominating possession for large periods at a ground that really did feel like a pre-season venue.

Saints could head into the small bar behind one of the two sets of posts having picked up a dogged 21-13 victory during which patience was the watchword. While onlookers made the most of the alcohol supplies, Saints simply kept knocking at the door, with their pressure paying off thanks to tries from prop Denman and Manoa, along with five points from the boot of Myler and six from young fly half Sam Olver.

The two sides would meet again in two of the most memorable fixtures a few months later, but Saints had plenty of important hurdles to negotiate before then. The season was looming large on the horizon and winning was becoming a welcome habit.

Game one: Saturday, 7 September 2013: Northampton Saints 38 Exeter Chiefs 11 (Aviva Premiership – round one)

Saints: Foden; K Pisi (Elliott 70), G Pisi (Wilson 60), Burrell, North; Myler, L Dickson (Fotuali'i 56); Corbisiero (A Waller 60), Hartley (c) (Haywood 58), Mercey (Denman 60), Lawes (Clark 58), Day, Wood (Manoa 56), Dowson, Dickinson.

Exeter: Dollman; Jess, Whitten, Shoemark (Hill 56), James; Steenson (Slade 51), Thomas (Lewis 56); Sturgess (Moon 54), Yeandle (Whitehead 54), Tui (Rimmer 54), Mumm (c), Welch (Hayes 64), Johnson, Scaysbrook (White 51), Ewers.

Referee: JP Doyle

Attendance: 12,205

Tries: Saints: Dylan Hartley, Ken Pisi, Tom Wood, George Pisi, Samu Manoa. **Exeter:** Dean Mumm

Conversions: Saints: Stephen Myler (5)

Penalties: Saints: Stephen Myler. **Exeter:** Gareth Steenson (2)

As far as starts to the season go, Saints' was pretty exceptional.

They clicked into gear from kick-off to put their Aviva Premiership opener against Exeter to bed inside 35 minutes.

Four tries during that time secured a welcome five points to get the campaign up and running ahead of tricky trips to Harlequins and Gloucester.

And one of the highlights was the impact made by a couple of players who, a year ago, many fans may not have heard of.

Luther Burrell and Sam Dickinson ran the show, allying power with panache as they helped Saints on their way to a 38-11 success. While George North, Alex Corbisiero and Kahn Fotuali'i took top billing, the northern boys proved they can be headline acts too.

Centre Burrell was instrumental in the opening two scores, flinging a fantastic pass out to Dylan Hartley for the first before making a cutting break and teeing up Ken Pisi for the second.

No.8 Dickinson also wreaked havoc, blasting holes in the Exeter back line and almost getting on the scoresheet himself in a powerhouse performance.

Of course, it wasn't all about those two men, but their opening-game form shows just how strong this season's Saints squad is.

So strong, that Lions star North did not even have to register for his men to get maximum points from their opening fixture.

So strong that the likes of Samu Manoa and Fotuali'i could be left on the bench until 20 minutes from time.

So strong that some of the stodgy games at the Gardens last season seemed a lifetime away.

But, as Mallinder pointed out after the match, it's only one match of 22 in the marathon that is the Premiership season.

Trips to The Stoop and Kingsholm now lie in wait and you can bet your bottom dollar their residents will be out to stop the Saints hype.

But if the men in green, black and gold can continue at the pace at which they began their first game of the new season, there will be plenty more strong showings in the coming weeks.

While pre-season had undoubtedly been productive, Saints knew that reading anything into those results would have been foolhardy. So the mood in the camp after the Exeter game was one of quiet satisfaction that they had found their opening-day game so comfortable, that they were up and running and that their friendly wins were backed up by a victory when it mattered.

Mallinder was certainly a happy man when he appeared in the press room to give his first post-match interview of the season and he was delighted that his team had been able to maintain the momentum they had gathered in the build-up to the big league kick-off.

'It was very pleasing,' the director of rugby said. 'You can play pre-season games, run around a lot, do some weight training, but you don't quite know where you are until your first game. Generally, we've got to be pretty happy with that.'

The only blots on the copybook for Saints during the curtain-raiser were yellow cards for Dowson and Lawes and Mallinder quickly made a point of stressing that discipline needed to improve, especially with back-to-back away games to come.

Saints knew they would be put under pressure by Harlequins at The Stoop on the following Friday and a mental note was made as they sought to ensure they would not be hampered by sin-binnings in the first away game of the new campaign.

A couple of days after the win against Exeter there was a different kind of away game to contend with as Saints' second team, the Wanderers, grabbed a welcome win at Welford Road.

Any win for Northampton over Leicester can be considered pleasing, especially given the rivalry between the two teams, but the favourable 23-15 scoreline was not the only positive.

Australian prop Ma'afu, who was starting to get up to speed and down to his fighting weight, was able to make his first appearance in Northampton colours, getting 65 minutes under his belt before being withdrawn, while Glenn Dickson, a Kiwi fly half recruited from Otago, also enjoyed a run-out.

Captain Ben Nutley had led the way in the success as he scored his side's opener and they went on to win it thanks to a penalty try plus points from the boot of Olver and new boy Dickson.

Everything was going swimmingly for Saints as a club at the start of the new season. They were in high spirits having refused to taste defeat during pre-season, the Premiership opener and the second-team clash with Tigers.

And they knew they would need to be in good shape for a clash with a Harlequins side who they had beaten in just one of the past seven encounters between the clubs. In fact, Saints had not won at The Stoop since September 2010.

Nevertheless, buoyed by the fact that they had been largely untested by Exeter and having seen Quins pushed all the way in their win against Wasps on the same weekend, Saints had every reason to be confident.

A game at Harlequins was exactly the kind of contest the likes of Corbisiero, Fotuali'i and North had been brought in to help their new club win. And Saints already had pedigree on their travels from the previous campaign, having claimed notable successes at Wasps and Saracens towards the back end of it.

The club were on the crest of a wave, but, after a sunny start to the season in Northampton, they would soon need to show just how adept they were at dealing with some south-west London water torture.

Game two: Friday, 13 September 2013: Harlequins 6 Northampton Saints 13 (Aviva Premiership – round two)

Harlequins: Brown; Williams (Smith 62), Lowe, Casson (Dickson 73), Monye; Evans (Botica 59), Care; Marler (Lambert 59), Gray (Buchanan 14), Doran-Jones (Collier 54), Merrick (Guest 64), Robson (c), Fa'asavalu (Wallace 68), Robshaw, Easter.

Saints: Foden; K Pisi (Elliott 58), Wilson, Burrell, North; Myler, Fotuali'i (L Dickson 58); Corbisiero (A Waller 62), Hartley (c), Mercey (Denman 45), Lawes (Dickinson 43), Day, Wood, Clark (Dowson 58), Manoa.

Referee: Andrew Small

Attendance: 11,498

Try: Saints: James Wilson

Conversion: Saints: Stephen Myler

Penalties: Saints: Stephen Myler (2). **Harlequins:** Nick Evans (2)

On the night BT Sport chose to broadcast their game to the nation for free, Saints may not have won too many new fans.

But Friday's success at The Stoop was one for those who have been behind the team since September 2010, the last time Northampton won at Harlequins.

It wasn't a pretty performance. In fact, at times, it was downright ugly. But it was so effective. Saints ground out a victory in the south-west London mudbath and how good it felt for those supporters who have seen their team lose so many close encounters with Quins in recent years.

In 2012, it was the last-gasp Premiership semi-final heartache, surrendering an eight-point lead in the final 13 minutes of the game to miss out on a place in the Premiership showpiece.

Last season, in a dead rubber, Saints were edged out by three points despite a spirited showing.

But this time was different. The line was in sight and no one was stopping Jim Mallinder's men from making it.

James Wilson, the man for all weathers, and most backline positions, was the match-winner, showing great intelligence to bend his run and latch on to a pass to slide over in the corner.

And George North also showed his immense worth with a rambunctious run that saw him hold off three men and put his side in enemy territory before the crucial try was scored.

However, this was mainly a game for the forwards. A real power struggle, eventually won by Dorian West's well-drilled pack. It is far too early to say that on nights like these champions are made, but Saints are certainly displaying the qualities required of a team who can challenge.

In the space of six days, they have shown they can ally silk with steel, using style to see off Exeter Chiefs and strength to shoot down Quins. Plenty more tough challenges await, and many will be far more aesthetically pleasing than this, but few will be as satisfying for those of a Saints persuasion.

On Friday 13, 'ugly' was the buzzword for Mallinder after the match, but though the performance was about as pretty as Freddy Krueger, this was no nightmare for Saints.

Everyone involved knew that this was the kind of win teams destined for greatness come away with because although it was monsoon season in London, Saints simply rolled up their sleeves, stuck on the armbands and battled against the tide to claim precious points on the road.

'You've got to accept you're going to get these nights,' Mallinder said. 'Against Exeter, it was a dry day, we played well and scored some good, open tries, but here we knew we wouldn't be able to play too much rugby.

'It's all about getting your set piece right, getting your kicking game right and once you get into their third, taking your opportunities, whether that's tries or kicking the goals.

'To do well in the Premiership, you need variety in your game. That's being able to play with 15 men, use the backs and a good passing game, but you need your set piece and to be able to play a territorial game at times. Nights like this, it's very sensible.

'They've got two good half-backs [Nick Evans and Danny Care] who have, in the past, punished us with their kicking game – I remember a close game we lost to Harlequins at home a couple of years ago where their half-backs played really well and beat us. It was good to come down here and to win in an ugly but nice way.'

Mallinder was well aware of how important it was to get that first away win under the belt and keep the feel-good factor flowing ahead of another away game, against Gloucester, on the following weekend.

More good news came in the form of key summer signings, with distinct signs that the new men were settling in.

North's run that set up Wilson's try was the kind of moment of magic that had made Saints desperately pursue the former Scarlets wing, while loosehead prop Corbisiero was key in a huge forward effort.

Players who had already cemented themselves at the club also made their mark, with Wilson's ability to deal with the torrential conditions so vital in securing the success.

Attack coach King had hinted at changes ahead of the game and his words proved not to be hollow as the likes of Wilson and Fotuali'i were handed starts, showing Saints wouldn't rest on their laurels.

And clearly a strong team bond had already been fostered, as the players who had dropped to the bench came on and made an impact, with Fotuali'i later hailing his side's super-subs.

'It's pretty exciting being named in the starting team and it's always good to have a win,' Fotuali'i said, having just dried out following his first Premiership start.

'From what I've heard it's always tough to come here. Harlequins are a quality side and top-four contenders, and especially in these conditions, it could have gone either way.

'Credit to our boys and the bench who came on really stood up and gave that impact that we needed.'

However, while the compliments were flying around and the players were rightly patting each other on the back following a stirring away win, this was just the start. Two wins may have been earned, but there was an awareness that with big statements comes a need to back them up.

Saints recognised they had more sizeable hurdles to negotiate in the weeks that followed, with a game at Leicester looming large on the horizon.

Consequently, Burrell, who had caught the eye in the opening two games, said: 'We know what it's like to go away from home and play – you've got to find that extra edge. Last year we were good on the road and it's just about trying to back that up this year.

'To go to a place like Harlequins and win in conditions like that is massive, so a massive pat on the back for the boys.

31

'There's been a lot of talk about us not being able to beat teams in the top four, but we don't really read too much into that.

'We take each game as it comes and to get a victory at Harlequins, who were title-winners a couple of years ago, is a massive success for us and we'll take it.'

And on the subject of the developing team spirit, the barrel-chested centre added: 'It's a good craic in the changing room. There's a good vibe at the club and we're trying to build that. We want to be mates on and off the field.

'We've got each other's backs at the end of the day and we'll take that. We're not over-confident. We've got some good players. Stevie Myler's really stepped up to the mark again this season, directing the boys around the park.

'We've got to take it week by week and keep getting these victories away from home.'

That was very much the view coming from the director of rugby's office, too, with Mallinder long enough in the tooth to know that two wins would not make a season.

'We can't [get carried away],' Mallinder had insisted. 'It would be ridiculous. It's only two games that we've played.

'It's fantastic to go to Harlequins and win because they've got aspirations to win the Premiership, like we have.

'It's good we got our win, but we've got Gloucester away on Saturday and we'll focus on that.'

Mallinder would never have been expected to hype his team up too much as he is a character who, win or lose, is often unmoved. He would give little away, and that was what Saints supporters had come to expect.

Nevertheless, it could be seen that progress was being made, on and off the pitch. Two days after the Harlequins win, Hewitt was officially named as Northampton chairman, converting his temporary role into a permanent one.

He expressed what a 'fantastic honour' it was for him to succeed the late Leon Barwell and looked forward to carrying on the fine work done by the Barwell family as a whole.

Saints now had the stability of having a guaranteed figurehead who they hoped would continue the strong traditions at the club. Later in the day it was back to the action as the Wanderers gave Hewitt a welcome present with an eight-try 52-26 success against Worcester Cavaliers.

Like the first team, the second string had secured a second win in as many games, displaying the depth in the squad as Kiwi second row Verbakel, signed from Otago during the summer, was joined on the scoresheet by Teimana Harrison, van Velze, Tom Collins, Ethan Waller, Alex Woolford and Howard Packman.

While the likes of Harrison and Collins showed that the future was indeed very bright at the Gardens, back in the present, Saints were boosted by the news that Lawes and Tom Mercey would be fit to face Gloucester at the weekend.

Their power would be key to claiming a win at Kingsholm as Saints sought to continue a strong start to the season up front.

Forwards coach Dorian West had expressed his delight at how the team had adapted to new scrum laws, which had seen 'crouch, bind, set' instructions introduced, with front rows having to bind before engaging and packs unable to push until the referee was happy.

Referees were expected to insist the ball was put in straight and the hookers were told they had to hook the ball, something that had been reduced during the previous ten years.

Saints had shown they were fast learners as they had not lost a scrum in their opening two games, prompting West to say: 'We haven't had too many problems with scrums so far.

'On the whole, I think it's gone pretty well. I think it's been positive.'

But those words were to come back to haunt Saints just a few days later.

Game three: Saturday, 21 September 2013: Gloucester 26 Northampton Saints 24 (Aviva Premiership – round three)

Gloucester: Cook; Sharples (May 75), Trinder, Twelvetrees, Simpson-Daniel; Burns (Tindall 68), Cowan (Robson 75); Murphy (Thomas 67), Dawidiuk, Harden (Knight 67), Savage (c) (James 67), Stooke, Kvesic, Qera (Morgan 64), Kalamafoni.

Saints: Foden; Elliott, Wilson (G Pisi 46), Burrell, North; Myler, Fotuali'i (L Dickson 54); A Waller (E Waller 67), Hartley (c) (Haywood 73), Mercey (Denman 67), Manoa (Dowson 63), Day, Wood, Clark, Dickinson (van Velze 67).

Referee: Martin Fox

Attendance: 12,688

Tries: Saints: Ben Foden, Samu Manoa, Jamie Elliott. **Gloucester:** Charlie Sharples, Billy Twelvetrees, Elliott Stooke

Conversions: Saints: Stephen Myler (3). **Gloucester:** Freddie Burns

Penalties: Saints: Stephen Myler. **Gloucester:** Freddie Burns (2), Billy Twelvetrees

---

Forty-five minutes after Saints had been kicked in the nether regions at Kingsholm, Jim Mallinder walked into the Gloucester press room.

The Northampton director of rugby was a picture of calm as he prepared to give his post-match interview to the written media.

To those who had seen his frustration-fuelled reaction when Gloucester had been awarded a late penalty, that may have been a surprise.

But Mallinder has been here before with Saints and, on reflection, he will be well aware that as hard to take as the decision was, it wasn't life or death in terms of his team's season. They have picked up ten points from their first three games, including a total of five from trips to Harlequins and Gloucester.

Most teams will struggle to take a single point from those fixtures, so Saints can be proud of their efforts there.

Another thing that must be remembered is that Mallinder steered his men to five successive wins at the start of the previous campaign, including one at Kingsholm. They went on to finish fourth, needing to step up to the plate at Saracens to make the Aviva Premiership Final.

The season is not decided on one result in September, though the three lost points could of course come back to haunt the club in the race for the top two.

Generally, though, it is often the case that these things even themselves out over the course of the season, and Mallinder was not prepared to brood for too long.

Admirably, he made it clear that his side could, and should, have done things better at Kingsholm, and they will now be focusing on seeing off Sale on Friday night.

As for Gloucester, they put in a gargantuan performance on Saturday and are far better than their opening two defeats had suggested.

They dominated possession for long spells against Saints, who showed their title credentials with some defiant defending and ruthless finishing on the road.

It was almost the perfect away performance as they soaked up pressure before scoring a picture-book try late on to set up a likely win.

George North's rampaging run down the left, beating three men, and Calum Clark's ability to find Jamie Elliott produced a moment that will live long in the memory.

Indeed, some are already talking about a try of the season contender – and few would argue.

It should have been the match-winning try and would have been, but for Fox's intervention.

The referee failed to spot a clear offside and then compounded that error with a scrum call that will leave even those of a Gloucester persuasion scratching their heads in disbelief.

To Twelvetrees' immense credit, with all the hubbub surrounding his kick, he bisected the posts well and the Cherry and Whites had the win.

It was a major boost for them and will surely kick-start their season.

But Saints will remain unbowed. They have not been broken by one swing of Twelvetrees' boot.

Instead, Mallinder, who says he looks at fixtures in blocks, will be happy with his side's work so far.

His wry smile in the Kingsholm press room said it all.

Injuries can cost sides dear at crucial moments, but you perhaps wouldn't think one sustained by a referee could be such a hammer blow to a side. That was very much the case for Saints at a sun-drenched Kingsholm as their hopes of registering a third successive win wilted in the West Country.

Martin Fox had been drafted in as a late replacement for Greg Garner, who was initially named as the man in the middle for the Premiership scrap at Gloucester. Garner had sustained an injury the day before the game and was forced to withdraw.

For Saints, it was an issue, as they had typically been a fan of how Garner refereed scrums, with West even hailing him as 'one of the best' after a 27-18 win at Worcester in February 2013. That was high praise indeed, especially as it came from a man regarded as one of the best forwards coaches in Europe after Northampton based their run to the 2011 Heineken Cup Final on scrum strength.

But they were not to find Fox as much to their liking as one blow of his whistle allowed Billy Twelvetrees to stick the boot in, bisecting the posts to spark wild scenes of celebration at Kingsholm. Mallinder had already headed down to the touchline by the time the penalty was awarded and his face, and reaction, told the tale for Saints.

'I've taken my frustration out on what was by the side of the pitch. Thankfully it wasn't Dorian West!' he said, in a more upbeat manner than expected after the game.

'We came close. We need to make sure every time we play a big team, we come close. We'll win some and we'll lose some.

'If we keep winning our home games that should see us in a good position come the end of the season.'

Mallinder and his players felt that Fox was wrong to give Gloucester the put-in on the third reset scrum. Saints felt it should have been their ball, but the Cherry and Whites seized possession and seized their moment when the decision went their way.

Austin Healey, who was commentating for BT Sport, suggested Fox had manufactured the penalty, but Mallinder, to his credit, was far more magnanimous, even if he did not agree with the decision that cost his team the match.

'It's a shame when games are decided by the referee in the last couple of minutes,' Mallinder said.

'We were disappointed when we had the change of referee at short notice, but sometimes that happens. As I said to the lads in the changing room, we've got to make sure we control what we can control. The refs are out of our hands. We've got to make sure of the parts of our game we can be more accurate with.

'We started well but they came back and the crowd had a big effect. You've got to make sure you're very accurate in everything you do. You've got to try to put the referee out of the equation.'

Saints thought they had done that when Elliott scored what was to eventually be voted the Premiership's try of the season. It was a stunning score, good enough to eclipse efforts from Christian Wade, Nick Abendanon, Kelly Brown, Logovi'i Mulipola and Dean Mumm, who were all shortlisted for the ITV-sponsored award.

However, it wasn't to be good enough to earn victory for Saints, who Foden felt had played it too safe as they were penned in by Gloucester for long periods

'I think we need to take more risks and play a bit more expansive rugby,' the England international had said. 'If we get the ball into George North's hands and Future's [Jamie Elliott] hands we'll cause teams problems.

'I think we played it a bit safe at Gloucester. There are plenty of things to work on for us as a side.

'In the second half, we spent most of it in our own half. We didn't exit very well and we put ourselves under a lot of pressure.

'There's plenty of things to work on. We've gone away, taken some positives out of the game and we're looking forward to putting things right on Friday against Sale.'

As Foden alluded to, North had not necessarily had as much of the ball as he would have liked in the games at Harlequins and Gloucester, with the juggernaut wing forced to feed off broken-field chances. However, he had shown enough striking glimpses to get Saints supporters off their seats and the following Friday's game against Sale Sharks appeared to present an opportunity for the behemoth to open his account at his new club.

Game four: Friday, 27 September 2013: Northampton Saints 33 Sale Sharks 14 (Aviva Premiership – round four)

Saints: Foden; Elliott, G Pisi (Wilson 61), Burrell, North (K Pisi 67); Myler, L Dickson (Fotuali'i 60); Corbisiero (A Waller 60), Hartley

(c) (Haywood 61), Mercey (Denman 60), Lawes (Wood 60), Day (Manoa 49), Clark, Dowson, Dickinson.

Sale Sharks: Arscott; Miller, Cueto, Forsyth, Brady (Ostrikov 69); Cipriani (Ford 67), Cliff (Fowles 67); Lewis-Roberts (Harrison 50), Taylor (Jones 50), Cobilas (Thomas 50), Kulemin (Mills 50), Paterson, Braid (c), Seymour, Easter.

Referee: David Rose

Attendance: 13,050

Tries: Saints: Luther Burrell, George North, George Pisi, Lee Dickson, Phil Dowson. **Sale:** Mark Cueto, Marc Jones

Conversions: Saints: Stephen Myler (4). **Sale:** Danny Cipriani, Joe Ford

---

Two home games, ten tries, two bonus-point wins – Saints are good value at the Gardens right now.

Friday night's win against Sale saw five scores, some sensational rugby and another comprehensive home success.

It's all a world away from some of the performances on Northampton turf during the early part of last season, when tries were far from flowing.

The team may have started with five wins from five at the beginning of the previous campaign, but there wasn't the level of excitement that exists currently.

Games were tighter, edgier and teams like Exeter and London Welsh pushed Saints all the way. There seemed to be a weight on the shoulders of the players.

Not now, though. Far from it. Despite the increase in expectation, the freedom is there for all to see. The belief is oozing from every pore. But it's not just since the summer; Saints have been sizzling since the back end of last season.

Then, teams such as London Irish and Sale were dispatched with ease at the Gardens, finding a Northampton team fizzing with belief hard to live with.

And Jim Mallinder's men have certainly picked up where they left off, systematically dismantling the Chiefs and, on Friday night, Sale again.

Saints went in at the break with three tries under their belts. And there was never any doubt they'd add to their tally after the interval.

Not because Sale were bad. No, unlike in April when they were already on the beach, Steve Diamond's men fought all the way.

They started strongly and refused to go away, despite shipping scores at regular intervals.

They even grabbed a try late on when it would have been easier to relax and think about that long journey back up the M6.

Saints, though, were just too good. They had too much confidence and too much power.

Yes, tougher tests lie in wait, especially in October when Leicester, Castres, Ospreys and Saracens provide the opposition.

But if the current wave of optimism and confidence remains, Saints fans will continue to get their money's worth.

Sure enough, North was to score his first Saints try in an entertaining encounter at Franklin's Gardens, where fans witnessed the real ambition of Mallinder's side, and their opponents.

The fact there wasn't a single three-pointer in the game showed just how keen Saints were to take it to the Sharks and sink them in a deluge of tries rather than kicks at goal.

Stephen Myler, leading the team out on his 200th appearance for Northampton, was required to boot the ball to the corner and add the extras to his side's impressive try count as they produced what was a high-tempo display that once again showed they meant business.

Earlier in the week, the second season ticket holders' forum was held, continuing the legacy of Leon Barwell, who had brought the club back together with a welcome meeting between supporters and the Northampton hierarchy in February 2013.

And whereas the mood was slightly fraught at that first gathering, the second was a walk in the park for Mallinder and Co. as they took to the stage at a time when the club was clearly on the up. The showing against Sale emphasised that, with the team showing its attacking intent and the likes of Burrell and North cashing in.

'We played outstanding rugby at times,' Mallinder said of the silky showing. 'Some of our tempo, some of our attacking play was very, very good.'

Sam Dickinson was also a happy man after the game as he continued to enjoy a seamless transition into the team after being unable to play a single first-team game during the previous season.

The big No.8 had arrived from Rotherham Titans during the summer of 2012, but an arm injury sustained towards the end of his time skippering the Championship club left him fearing his Saints deal would be taken away.

However, the club kept faith with the player and in the early games of this campaign he showed exactly why, with some towering performances in a hugely impressive back row that also included the likes of Wood, Calum Clark, Dowson and Samu Manoa.

After the win against Sale, Dickinson began to reflect on the journey he had been on and it was a pleasure to listen to the approachable northern lad.

'Maybe spending all my time last year training helped me out a little bit,' Dickinson said. 'A lot of credit is due to Moseley, who I went on loan with and played a fair few games for last year.

'I've said to a number of people coming into this team that you look around, look at the names we've got and it's easy to slot in. It's as much credit to the team around me.'

Dickinson was even rivalling reigning player of the year Manoa for a place in the team, but, in typically modest fashion, he played down suggestions that he might keep the USA star out of the first 15, preferring to focus on the team ethic that continued to build.

'I'm not looking at who's in and out, I'm happy just to be playing,' Dickinson had added. 'He [Manoa] is a massive guy to have around and he does a hell of a job when he's on the pitch as well so there's a one-squad mentality. Everyone's happy that we're winning.

'There's lots of smiles knocking around. I feel we're playing a good brand of rugby, it's exciting. We play wide when we can, we take our opportunities and it's putting smiles on everyone's faces.'

But the Saints players knew that the smiles would be even broader if they were able to win the following weekend at a venue their club had not claimed victory at since 2007, when Mark Robinson's magnificent individual effort earned a 10-9 win against Leicester Tigers at Welford Road.

The week leading up to the latest instalment of the East Midlands derby, and the first meeting since Saints' defeat to Tigers in the 2013 Premiership Final, was packed with appraisals and challenges.

Mallinder saluted Lee Dickson's 'fantastic' energy as the scrum half's battle with Fotuali'i for the Saints No.9 shirt continued to hot up, Hartley insisted his side still had plenty of improving to do and Mallinder urged his team to maintain their form through the 'difficulties' ahead.

The key to Saints negotiating those obstacles Mallinder spoke of was belief. Belief that they could maintain their good run. Belief that they could finally beat their old foes in the Leicester backyard.

Corbisiero, one of the men brought in to give the club the confidence, quality and composure to pass tests they had previously failed, spoke eloquently about what he and his team-mates needed to do to end a run of eight games without victory against the Tigers.

'I think we've just got to focus on our own game,' Corbisiero said in his typically cool manner. 'Leicester are a great side, they've been at the top of European rugby for a reason. They're a well-drilled, good set-piece, good, talented team with some try scorers and some flair in there but we've got a decent defence ourselves. We need to confront them on the battleground areas and play our game. We don't need to do anything different to what we have been doing, we just need to match them.'

The man charged with selecting the team to match and eventually overcome Leicester was Mallinder, who admitted it would be a 'great' personal fillip to finally end his winless run at Welford Road. The director of rugby would have a fully fit squad to choose from, handing him and his coaches some selection headaches in the build-up to the big game. However, it all came back to that belief, and Mallinder knew that whatever team he picked must have full confidence that they could conquer the home of the Tigers.

'We'll pick a side to go up there and win,' said a bullish Mallinder. 'We've got good players who are on form. They all want to play. We can't start everyone but we've got some tough games coming up with the Heineken Cup following on.

'We'll pick a side we think is strong enough to go and win at Welford Road. We've got to go there and take them on.'

As it turned out, Mallinder opted to make two changes to his side, with big-hitters Manoa and Wood drafted in to add bulk to the pack in place of Christian Day and Clark.

While Saints were oozing confidence, Leicester were cautious, with Tigers boss Richard Cockerill insisting his team would face a 'more rounded' rival than they had done in a dominant run against Northampton during previous meetings.

However, Cockerill would not be able to influence events on the field from his typical vantage point as he was still feeling the effect of a nine-game touchline ban dished out for haranguing fourth official Stuart Terheege during the fiery Premiership Final against Saints earlier in the year.

Cockerill had complained about Courtney Lawes' hit on Toby Flood during the first half and it was later decided that he would not be able to return to full matchday duties until 18 October, meaning he would have to sit in a dark corner of Welford Road to watch his team take on their traditional adversaries.

Mallinder fielded questions about the ban with a mixture of glee and barbed words, knowing Cockerill wouldn't fade quietly into the background on derby day.

'Although he won't be sat in his little box behind his screen shouting away, I'm sure he'll be in some little corner of Welford Road shouting at the referee,' Mallinder said, smirking.

It prompted smiles from the assembled media, knowing of the history between the two clubs, and provided the perfect appetiser for what was ahead: another frantic, feisty, exhilarating East Midlands derby.

Game five: Saturday, 5 October 2013: Leicester Tigers 19 Northampton Saints 19 (Aviva Premiership – round five)

Leicester: Scully; Morris, Goneva, Allen (Bowden 70), Thompstone; Flood, B Youngs (Mele 70); Mulipola, T Youngs, Cole, Deacon, Kitchener, Slater, Salvi, Crane.

Saints: Foden; Elliott, G Pisi, Burrell (Wilson 70), North; Myler, L Dickson; Corbisiero (A Waller 64), Hartley (c), Mercey (Denman 64), Manoa, Lawes, Wood, Dowson, Dickinson.

Referee: JP Doyle

Attendance: 23,891

Tries: Leicester: Ed Slater. **Saints:** Alex Corbisiero

Conversions: Leicester: Toby Flood. **Saints:** Stephen Myler

Penalties: Leicester: Toby Flood (4). **Saints:** Stephen Myler (4)

Jim Mallinder wanted Saints to take the game to Tigers on derby day – and he got his wish.

For long spells, the away side dictated proceedings, displaying the ever-increasing confidence among their phalanx of talented backs.

Saints went toe to toe with Tigers on their own turf. It wasn't the first time, but on this occasion there was a real threat to the home team.

And, with ten minutes to go, Mallinder's men looked set to end a winless run at Welford Road which stretches back to 2007.

But, to their credit, Tigers came roaring back. That is, of course, what champion teams do. They don't give up, even when the mountain seems too steep to climb.

Toby Flood showcased his class to take the game by the scruff of the neck in the final exchanges, just as Stephen Myler had been doing for prolonged periods.

And, in the end, Tigers had two points that looked hugely unlikely at various stages, especially when Alex Corbisiero burrowed his way over the line on 46 minutes.

Saints, though, can take great heart from the way they performed. They looked Tigers in the eye and refused to blink first.

The best illustration of that came during the first half when Myler turned down a kickable penalty, instead booting the ball to the corner. Saints weren't at Welford Road to say 'thank you' to Leicester for giving them the occasional three points.

This is not a Northampton team prepared to take the scraps, it wants to dine at the top table and feast on the best food its rivals have to offer.

Saints weren't able to convert the line-out in a promising position, but, at 3-0 up, they had signalled their intent.

And, led by the likes of Courtney Lawes and Sam Dickinson, who put in gargantuan performances, they were to continue in that vein.

That was until Tigers eventually found their feet late on and began to turn the screw, backed by the fervent home faithful.

Saints will know they should have seen the game out, and two yellow cards during the course of it didn't do them any favours.

Luther Burrell and, with ten minutes to go, Lawes were sent to the bin and, right or wrong, that is now seven yellow cards in five games this season.

Mallinder made a point of saying his side couldn't afford to sustain sin-binnings at Welford Road.

And, although they coped well without Burrell, being shorn of man of the match Lawes late on undoubtedly had a big impact.

Lawes had risen to the task of calling the line-outs in the absence of Christian Day and, even though Tigers had Louis Deacon binned at the same time, his absence was vital.

The ability to stop sides scoring without men getting on the wrong side of the referee is something Saints must work on in the weeks and months to come.

Overall, though, Saturday's showing elicited far more positives than negatives.

At the end of last season and the start of this one, Northampton have shown they can go to the toughest venues and push their hosts to breaking point.

Now they'll need to do it all again in the Heineken Cup next weekend, when Castres, a side who beat Saints in the pool stages last season, provide the opposition.

In the grand scheme of the season, a win there is more important than one at Tigers.

Wins on the road in the short European format will be crucial with the pool Saints have been presented with – Ospreys and Leinster also lie in wait – and flaying the French would be a great way to start.

And if they can iron out those disciplinary problems and play to the level they did at Welford Road on Saturday, Mallinder will know his men have every chance.

'A moral victory.' That was what Mallinder felt this was for Northampton. Predictably, his reaction was one of pride tinged with disappointment because he had seen his men carry out their plan almost to the letter until they were finally undone late on.

They had done what he wanted. They had stood up to a Leicester team shorn of the scourge of Saints, Manu Tuilagi, and inspirational forward Tom Croft. Not only that, but they had been better than the home side for long periods of the match.

Corbisiero converted his pre-match confidence into a try and Saints held the upper hand on a ground they had been so used to having their noses shoved into. Referee Barnes, so often a man in the spotlight during East Midlands derbies, was nowhere to be seen on this occasion and it all felt a little different.

Just like during the second half of the Premiership Final meeting between the teams, there was a fearlessness about Saints and a nervousness about Leicester. Cockerill, who spent this game in a box behind a glass screen due to his touchline ban, saw his trepidation about the fixture mirrored by his team's fans.

Had they lost, Leicester could have had no complaints, especially due to the sheer volume of possession Saints had during the formative stages of the match. But, as they always do, Leicester came on strong towards the end, and it was to be enough to unpick a side who had gallantly charged into a 19-9 lead.

Ed Slater's 76th-minute try and Flood's conversion secured a share of the spoils for the home side, who threatened to really rub salt in the wounds and win it in the final seconds of the match. However, Saints ensured they would come away with something for all of their efforts and they were left to think about what might have been as they came as close to breaking what was now a six-year hoodoo as they ever had before.

Mallinder talked about how it was 'here for winning' and spoke about the 'pressure' his team applied, but he felt Tigers would be the happier because of the hole they had found themselves in before Slater's late score.

A win would have been the perfect way to round off the block of five Premiership games. It would have given Saints an extra boost ahead of the European excursion that lay in wait the following weekend. However, Mallinder still felt his team was 'in good shape' and he knew that by winning at Harlequins and pushing Tigers to the edge, his side had shown they could mix it with opposition teams who had seemed to have their number in previous years.

Academy graduate Lawes summed the improvement up as he stated: 'I don't think we've had a team this good, powerful and organised for a long, long time. It certainly showed in the game against Harlequins as well; we're winning and drawing at difficult places.

'We're only going to get better as a team. We've got a lot of new faces and hopefully we can just keep it going and keep building.'

While the likes of Corbisiero and North were adding undoubted quality to that building process, other, less well known players had been catching the eye. Burrell's and September player of the month Dickinson's roles in Saints' early-season charge had not gone unnoticed, especially by England head coach Stuart Lancaster, who had saluted the duo.

Wood also remained on Lancaster's radar, with the hard-working flanker being tipped to take over the captaincy of the national team, having led them to a series victory in Argentina during the summer.

But for now, the sights of Saints' star men were trained on rediscovering the clinical streak they showed in the win at Harlequins and in the demolition of Sale in time for the first stop on the team's European journey.

The name of Northampton had been placed in what was widely seen as the 'pool of death', with Castres, Leinster and Ospreys providing the opposition. Castres were the reigning French champions, Leinster were PRO12 holders and Ospreys had plenty of threats of their own.

First up for Saints was a trip to the home of the French team, who were familiar foes for Mallinder's men. Northampton and Castres had met in the pool stages of the previous three Heineken Cup campaigns, with the Top 14 outfit claiming victory in a meeting in Toulouse a year earlier.

As they had at Leicester a week earlier, Saints had shown flashes of their capabilities in that clash, but they had been unable to get the win they wanted. Consequently, they knew they must bring back the guillotine-sharp edge that had cut Exeter, Harlequins and Sale apart earlier in the season to get their European campaign off to a flying start at Stade Pierre Antoine.

Game six: Saturday, 12 October 2013: Castres Olympique 19 Northampton Saints 13 (Heineken Cup pool stages – game one)

Castres: Palis; Martial, Cabannes, Lamerat, Evans; Tales (c), Kockott; Lazar, Mach (Rallier 70), Peikrishvili (Wihongi 51), Gray, Capo-Ortega, Bornman, Faasalele (Wannenburg 59), Claassen.

Saints: Foden; K Pisi (Elliott 65), G Pisi, Burrell, North (Wilson 69); Myler, Fotuali'i (L Dickson 59); Corbisiero (A Waller 67), Hartley (c), Ma'afu (Mercey 59), Lawes, Day (Dowson 65), Wood, Clark, Dickinson (Manoa 59).

Referee: George Clancy

Attendance: 7,624

Tries: Castres: Romain Martial. **Saints:** Dylan Hartley

Conversions: Castres: Rory Kockott. **Saints:** Stephen Myler

Penalties: Castres: Rory Kockott (4). **Saints:** Stephen Myler (2)

Regrets, Saints would have had a few when they landed back at Luton Airport on Sunday afternoon. Because while one losing bonus point was safely tucked away in the suitcase, three more remained on the Stade Pierre Antoine pitch.

Saints went to Castres and stood up to the challenge presented by the French champions.

In fact, they did more than stand up. They stood up and shouted at the top of their voice, but yet they weren't heard when it mattered.

Chances came and went, while Castres were more clinical as they took every opportunity presented to them.

Romain Martial's try, handed to him on a plate by Luther Burrell's pass, and 14 points from the metronome that is Rory Kockott was the sum total of their forays into Saints territory.

The game was largely played in the French team's half, but, to their credit, they stuck manfully to their task, defending as Saints endeavoured to knock the door down.

Whether Castres will hold out with such strength in the later rounds of the competition should they start to struggle remains to be seen.

But they certainly irked a Northampton team, who, aside from skipper Dylan Hartley's opportunistic try, lacked any real ruthlessness in enemy territory.

It was a similar story to the one at Leicester a week earlier as they had the possession to comfortably win the game. But when it mattered, they were unable to make it pay.

Supporters summed it up after the game, with social networking sites saturated with one word: Frustration.

'Why do I support the most frustrating rugby team on the whole planet,' tweeted one supporter.

'Saints are talented, powerful, dominant, experienced ... & the most frustrating team around!' added another.

And Jim Mallinder and Hartley didn't waste any time in making similar statements during their post-match interviews.

Neither man was too downbeat, though. They know there is a long way to go in this competition. Five more games that will decide their European fate.

But a big dollop of pressure has been placed on Sunday's showdown with Ospreys at Franklin's Gardens.

The Welsh side were opening-day casualties too, being hurt at home by Leinster, who claimed a 19-9 win at the Liberty Stadium.

It's first blood to the Irish and French, while Saints were left to wonder what might have been on their return to English soil.

As it turned out, Saints had not learned their Leicester lesson, and they were to fail their French test, to the palpable frustration of everyone of a green, black and gold persuasion.

The monotonous drum beat provided by the home supporters at Stade Pierre Antoine weighed heavy on Northampton shoulders as their team failed to get off to the flying start Myler had called for in the days leading up to the Saturday evening showdown.

Instead, they were left to rue a lack of efficiency at both ends of the field, with a rare errant pass from Burrell, who was to get an England call the following week, gifting Castres a precious try in a game when defences were firmly on top.

Just as at Leicester, Saints had hit the self-destruct button late on – not in the concession of points at the death, but in their failure to score them, with Hartley's try the only time they managed to penetrate a home rearguard who relished keeping their English opponents at arm's length to earn a vital opening-day win. Hartley certainly saw the similarities with events at Welford Road as he conducted an interview close to the tunnel in the minutes after the game.

'We certainly missed an opportunity,' he said. 'Going to Leicester as well and being in the lead in that game, thinking that if we close it out it would be four points, and it was a bit like that in this game.

'Castres were not French champions for nothing, they've got a proud home record and it wasn't going to be easy, but we really thought we could come here and take four points.'

Mallinder mirrored his captain's frustration as he too stepped forward for media duties, but he was trying to remain upbeat, despite knowing the failure to take at least four points from the game could cost his team as the 'pool of death' progressed.

'We're frustrated that we couldn't get a win, but it is a point and we're still in the competition,' Mallinder said. 'There's six games in this competition and what you must do is win your home games so it makes it essential that we win next week's game against Ospreys.'

One positive that Mallinder could take into that Ospreys game came in the form of Australian prop Ma'afu. The powerhouse had been parachuted into the team to steady a scrum that creaked badly at Welford Road a week earlier and he was able to have the desired effect.

The experienced international, who had been involved in the Wanderers' humbling 40-19 defeat to Sale Jets at Heywood Road earlier in the week, donned a broad smile as he discussed the game in the strange setting of a washing room after the match at the Stade Pierre Antoine, and he had every right to smile. His work up front had laid a solid foundation for the season ahead and though he was continuing to work on his fitness, he looked like he had settled in nicely under the tuition of forwards coach West.

However, while Ma'afu was now looking forward to a first start at Franklin's Gardens in the vital game against the Ospreys on the following weekend, Saints were harbouring worries over the fitness of their Lions duo.

North had suffered a jaw injury at Castres, while Corbisiero was definitely out after it was confirmed that he needed to have fluid drained from his knee and would be sidelined for a number of weeks.

Saints could ill afford such casualties with the Castres defeat having ramped up the pressure ahead of what promised to be a hugely difficult encounter against a bullish Ospreys team, but there was confidence in the Northampton camp that they could cope.

In fact, some players were just craving a chance to play, with Clark admitting that the rotation policy that had been employed up to that point in the season had been 'hard to get your head around'.

The flanker had been fighting for a place in a back row packed with power and despite being disappointed that he wasn't starting every week, he was sure that the competition would only drive the club on to great things.

'It's hard to get your head around because it's something new to us, but you have to learn and take your chances when you get them,' Clark said bullishly. 'Whenever you're on the field you have to go as hard as you can because we have got a lot of depth in the back five so it's important we use it.

'In the short term you get annoyed, you're not quite sure what's going on in the coaches' minds, but in the long term that will drive us all on.

'You train alongside the blokes you're rotating with and you're getting a fair chance. When it comes to the big game it's the ones who have done the best with that chance who will get picked, so long term I think it's a really good thing.'

Saints certainly hoped Clark's confidence would be justified against Ospreys because, with back-to-back games against European powerhouses Leinster to come in December, they could not afford another episode like the one in Castres.

They would have to shuffle their cards accordingly to ensure that they packed a punch when the Welshmen arrived in Northampton on a Sunday afternoon saturated with suspense.

Game seven: Sunday, 20 October 2013: Northampton Saints 27 Ospreys 16 (Heineken Cup pool stages – game two)

Saints: Foden; Elliott (K Pisi 75), G Pisi, Burrell, North; Myler, L Dickson (Fotuali'i 63); A Waller (E Waller 70), Hartley (c) (Haywood 75), Ma'afu (Denman 58), Lawes, Day, Dowson (Clark 56), Wood, Manoa (van Velze 56).

Ospreys: Fussell; Hassler, Bishop (Lewis 70), Beck (Morgan 72), Walker; Biggar, Habberfield; Bevington (D Jones 63), Hibbard (Baldwin 70), A Jones (Jarvis 54), A W Jones, King, R Jones (Ardron 54), Tipuric, Bearman (Allen 48).

Referee: Alain Rolland

Attendance: 13,182

Tries: Saints: Samu Manoa, Christian Day, Ben Foden. **Ospreys:** Dan Biggar

Conversions: Saints: Stephen Myler (3). **Ospreys:** Dan Biggar

Penalties: Saints: Stephen Myler (2). **Ospreys:** Dan Biggar (3)

Saints ended Sunday's game against Ospreys with two words in mind: Job done.

Because while the chance of a four-try bonus point went begging late on, Jim Mallinder's men had what they set out for, and that was a win.

An extra point would have been the icing on the cake, but they will be more than happy with taking a bite out of Ospreys in what was a must-win match for both teams.

And while the Welshmen need something of a miracle to progress now, as displayed by the reaction of players and coaches at the end, Saints are definitely still in the hunt.

Five points from the first two games have set them up nicely for what is likely to be a decisive double-header against Leinster, who top Pool 1 on eight points.

And they should not fear the Irish giants, going by the evidence provided by the opening scenes of this season's competition.

The key thing is, though, that Saints have at least given themselves a shot at making the knock-out stages for the first time since 2011, and they did it with a determined display on Sunday.

Ospreys were hurting after their defeat to Leinster and the noises coming out of their camp before the game were ominous.

They were desperate to put things right on the road, where they had won only two of their previous 18 Heineken Cup games. That they didn't is to Saints' immense credit. The men in green, black and gold won the battle at the breakdown on several occasions, forcing Ospreys to cough up possession.

And Saints also won the scrum showdown, which was made all the more impressive when you consider the pillars of strength in the opposition pack.

Ospreys boasted four Lions, but Saints at times made them look like kittens as Alex Waller came of age at loosehead and Salesi Ma'afu showed his worth on his home debut.

Waller has been waiting for his chance for a number of years, standing in the shadow of Soane Tonga'uiha and, this season, Alex Corbisiero, but how he seized his chance.

Credit must also go to young Mike Haywood, who came on as a blood replacement for skipper Dylan Hartley, faced up to Lions hooker Richard Hibbard and helped Saints score their first try.

Academy graduates Waller and Haywood helped their side get a shove on five metres out and Samu Manoa's run round the back from No.8 left Ospreys bamboozled.

It set Saints up and, led by gargantuan performances from Courtney Lawes and Dylan Hartley once more, they got the win they needed and the win they deserved.

For Ospreys, it may be game over. But for Saints it might just be game on in this season's Heineken Cup.

On occasion, Sunday afternoon games can be a bit flat at Franklin's Gardens, but this one certainly wasn't, and that was due to the fact there was so much riding on it for the Saints. Slipping on the Welsh banana skin simply wasn't an option for Mallinder's men and they produced a professional performance.

It got them back on track following the frustrations of Leicester and Castres and, all in all, they enjoyed their home comforts as their opponents' bout of travel sickness continued.

Ospreys had a woeful record in the Heineken Cup and it was to become two wins in 19 matches after this defeat at the hands of a Saints side who belied the absence of Corbisiero.

Alex Waller came in and had a Lion for lunch as he took Adam Jones to task in the scrum, helping to lay the foundations for a vital victory that kept his team alive and kicking ahead of the decisive December double against Leinster.

Mike Haywood also showed his worth when filling in for Hartley at times during the game and Saints, who were boosted by the presence of North, who shrugged off that jaw injury to face his countrymen, once again displayed their squad depth.

Not only that, but their frontline players stepped up and shouldered the pressure, with lofty lock Lawes the stand-out star on an afternoon when the Anglo-Welsh encounter went the way of the men from Northampton.

'He was sort of in and out of games in the past but now he's the complete player for the full game,' said a satisfied Mallinder of Lawes, who had been a beacon of light for his club amid some of the disappointment in the previous two games.

As man of the match, Lawes was thrust into the limelight after the game, when he was asked to give his views on his personal performances. The second row enforcer had some interesting things to say, admitting that not looking for pain was leading to plenty of gain.

'It always has been about getting a run of games,' the England man said. 'I'm staying fit and playing a lot smarter now, not trying to really hurt people. I'm looking after my shoulders and my body a bit more and it seems to be working.

'The fact that you're not looking for it means most of the time it comes to you anyway and that's something I've learned as I've got older, a bit more mature and a bit more experienced.

'I'm starting to enjoy my rugby and it's starting to come a bit easier, which is nice.'

It was certainly nice for Saints, who had boosted morale levels not only for future endeavours in Europe but also for the crucial Premiership clash that was to come on the following weekend.

Saracens were the team steeling themselves for a trip to the Gardens and they would be gunning for revenge in the first meeting with Saints since Mallinder's men upset the odds to prevail at Allianz Park in the previous season's Premiership play-off semi-final.

Events in the England camp would have a bearing on the big battle in Northampton, with Lancaster releasing players back to their clubs ahead of the upcoming autumn international series against Australia, Argentina and New Zealand.

Unsurprisingly, Lawes was one of seven Saints stars who had been named in a 34-man England squad, with Hartley, Lawes, Lee Dickson, Foden, Corbisiero and Wood, who was to miss out on the captaincy, which was given to Chris Robshaw, also involved.

To the delight of Mallinder, Foden and Burrell would be allowed to head back to the Gardens for the game against Saracens, who were bolstered by the return of full back Alex Goode.

However, there were still plenty of key men absent – Saints were also without North, who was called up by Wales – and question marks hung over the game, with supporters left wondering which club would be best placed to deal with their lengthy list of absentees in what remained a mouth-watering battle of two of England's finest teams.

Game eight: Saturday, 26 October 2013: Northampton Saints 41 Saracens 20 (Aviva Premiership – round six)

Saints: Foden (Wilson 67); K Pisi, G Pisi, Burrell (Waldouck 67), Elliott (Glynn 75); Myler, Fotuali'i; A Waller (E Waller 62), Haywood (McMillan 75), Ma'afu (Denman 58), Manoa (Nutley 67), Day, Clark, Dowson (c), Dickinson (van Velze 40).

Saracens: Goode; Tagicakibau (Bosch 55), Wyles, Taylor, Strettle; Mordt (Ransom 67), Wigglesworth (de Kock 55); Barrington (Auterac 67), Brits (George 55), Stevens (Johnston 55), Borthwick (c), Hargreaves (Botha 55), Brown, Burger (Wray 60), Joubert.

Referee: Tim Wigglesworth

Attendance: 13,474

Tries: Saints: Jamie Elliott, Samu Manoa, Ben Foden (2), Luther Burrell, Ken Pisi. **Saracens:** Duncan Taylor, Kelly Brown

Conversions: Saints: Stephen Myler (4). **Saracens:** Alex Goode (2)

Penalties: Saints: Stephen Myler. **Saracens:** Alex Goode (2)

The phrase 'strength in depth' is bandied about more freely than Christmas present ideas at this time of the year.

With international players being whisked away to represent their countries, teams are left needing to shuffle their pack.

All the talk in the lead-up to matches for sides who have lost key men is of how strong the squad is.

How the team can cope without five or six of its stellar names.

How much strength in depth there is.

And, just like with those Christmas presents, sometimes people are left disappointed.

Sometimes the players you have been told are capable of stepping up to the big time don't.

Saints fans have had their fair share of that anti-climactic feeling in previous seasons.

But they did not have it on Saturday.

Instead it was Saracens who ended up with the unsightly jumper knitted by an elderly relative, while Saints got their hands on a more coveted present: five points.

No George North. No Tom Wood. No Courtney Lawes. No Alex Corbisiero. No Dylan Hartley. No Lee Dickson. No problem.

Saints took it all in their stride, showed their strength in depth and marched to a huge success at Franklin's Gardens.

Saracens were left feeling bloated, sluggish and in need of a good lie down after this one. And their South African No.8 Ernst Joubert was left to rue his remarks ahead of the game. Because Joubert had used those three precious words, and they came back to bite him and his team.

'It's a bit of a shame that it's a game like Saracens against Northampton and there won't be the internationals there but there is so much strength in depth at this club,' he said.

'The players coming in are just as good as those who are missing and they are hungry to prove themselves because they maybe haven't had as much time on the field as they wanted.

'It's something that we pride ourselves on, having a big squad that means we can compete in different competitions and I think we are going to show that with the internationals away.'

The truth is, as Saints boss Jim Mallinder admitted after the game, you just never know how you will adapt to losing some of your best men. And it was clear that Northampton dealt with the absences better.

Alex Waller, who ate a Lion, Ospreys' Adam Jones, for breakfast six days earlier, ate another Lion, Matt Stevens, for lunch on this occasion. Mike Haywood, stepping into the sizeable shoes of Dylan Hartley, fronted up to Schalk Brits in a big way. And Samu Manoa, moving into the second row in the absence of Courtney Lawes, was simply sensational, capping a mammoth display with a stunning solo try.

Saints will need more of the same in the coming weeks, but finally they seem to have the strength in depth to set themselves up nicely for the festive period.

'You can look at it as they've got an opportunity on Saturday to put in a performance and put their hand up for the next few weeks.' That was what Saints coach Alan Dickens had said about Burrell and Foden following their release by England prior to this game.

And how Burrell and Foden stepped up on this occasion. Both players scored – Burrell once and Foden twice – as they hammered home their point to England boss Lancaster ahead of the following week's clash with Australia at Twickenham.

The in-form pair played crucial roles in a Saints team that showed Saracens just whose squad was best suited to dealing with an autumn period that would rob both title chasers of a number of stars.

Once again, the likes of Alex Waller and Haywood showed they could not only mix it with the best, but completely overpower them, as Northampton swatted aside their rivals in a six-try demolition.

Goode, like Burrell and Foden, did well, showing England head coach Lancaster what he was made of, but the full back's display was nowhere near enough to help save a Saracens side who never came close to dishing out the revenge they wanted for the previous season's semi-final defeat.

In fact, the Londoners were left stunned, having been out-thought and outclassed by a Saints team who played some Champagne rugby on their way to crushing the 100 per cent league record their rivals had previously enjoyed.

It was yet another statement, to add to the win at Harlequins and the draw with Leicester, and it saw Mallinder's men close the gap to summit side Saracens to a single point.

It showed the men from Northampton meant business and demonstrated that they had the squad to cope with any challenge that was thrown at them.

Mallinder was, understandably, purring in his praise of his team in the post-match interviews, labelling them 'clinical' as they inflicted Saracens' biggest defeat in four and a half years.

'It was pretty good, wasn't it?' said the Saints boss, who had seen his team take their tally of tries at the Gardens to 19 in just four games. 'To score 40-odd points against Saracens is pleasing.

'You never quite know how teams will react when they lose international players but what was really pleasing for us was that it was such a good squad effort.'

That squad effort Mallinder spoke of would step up a notch in the next few weeks as they were forced to negotiate another Premiership game before the glitz and glamour of England's top division was to be replaced by the less attractive LV= Cup.

With North still with Wales and five players – Lawes, Wood, Lee Dickson, Hartley and Foden – retained by England for the Australia game, Saints' squad was once again stretched for the trip to London Irish. In seeking to maintain consistency, only two changes were made, both of which were enforced, as Foden, who had been kept on by England, and the injured Elliott were replaced by Wilson and Premiership debutant Tom Collins respectively.

Prior to the game everyone of a Saints persuasion got the chance to watch their England boys in action, and Lancaster's team were to enjoy a super Saturday, hitting back to beat Australia 20-13 at Twickenham, where Lawes, Wood, Dickson and Hartley all stepped on to the hallowed turf for the first time since that agonising Premiership Final defeat to Leicester.

It was a much happier experience on this occasion and, a day later, their Saints team-mates travelled to Berkshire in a bid to banish a few of the club's other nagging demons by bagging a win of their own.

Game nine: Sunday, 3 November 2013: London Irish 14 Northampton Saints 19 (Aviva Premiership – round seven)

London Irish: O'Connor; Ojo, Mulchrone, Sheridan, Tagicakibau (Lewington 78); Humphreys, O'Leary (c) (Allinson 78); Yapp (Parr

49), Paice, Halavatau (Hagan 49), Gough, Evans, Cowan, Treviranus (Danaher 78), Hala'ufia (Low 56).

Saints: Wilson; K Pisi, G Pisi (Waldouck 62), Burrell, Collins; Myler, Fotuali'i; A Waller (E Waller 70), Haywood (McMillan 78), Ma'afu (Mercey 56), Manoa (Nutley 59), Day, Clark, Dowson (c), Dickinson (van Velze 27).

Referee: Andrew Small

Attendance: 7,247

Tries: London Irish: Sailosi Tagicakibau. **Saints:** James Wilson

Conversions: Saints: Stephen Myler

Penalties: London Irish: Ian Humphreys (3). **Saints:** Stephen Myler (4)

It was more the Glad Stad than the Mad Stad for Saints as they showed their strength at London Irish on Sunday.

They produced a performance that was the complete antithesis of the one 13 months earlier, when they were eviscerated by a rampant Exiles outfit.

This time there was no sloppy defending, no lack of defiance and no yard yielded without a fight.

Instead, Saints showed determination, guts and gusto as they delivered a fine away-day win.

Okay, so their attacking game didn't quite click into gear.

They didn't necessarily look like a team who have registered 19 tries in four home games this season.

But this clash wasn't at Franklin's Gardens.

It was at a ground where their hosts had lost just once in 2013.

Only Exeter Chiefs had previously come and gone with a win to their name.

And this was an Irish side boosted by the arrival of Australia star James O'Connor, who sparkled on debut.

The fact the full back's contribution wasn't a winning one owed much to Saints' rearguard action.

Every member of the team, from the youngest, Premiership debutant Tom Collins, to the oldest, inspirational skipper Phil Dowson, battled bravely to ensure the win.

The loss of eight players who would normally be in the starting shake-up wasn't allowed to have an effect.

This is a Northampton squad with a point to prove, desperate to show, this season, they can compete during international periods.

And they are certainly doing that as a superlative attacking showing against Saracens was backed up with a cogent defensive display against Irish.

Players such as James Wilson, in for England's Ben Foden, and Collins, replacing the injured Jamie Elliott, threw their bodies on the line for the cause.

The same could be said for Luther Burrell, who is knocking loudly on the England door after another thundering 80 minutes in Saints colours.

The big centre, often so threatening in attack, showed his worth going the other way with some huge, and crucial, hits.

He and Dowson typified Saints' effort and drive as they kept the heat on Saracens at the top of the table.

They have emerged from seven testing league fixtures with five wins and a draw, with the only defeat coming in unfortunate fashion at Gloucester.

It is a start containing far more substance than the one they enjoyed last season.

The mad moment at Irish last October showed there were flaws in Saints' squad.

This year, the glad-all-over feeling inspired by Sunday's win illustrates the opposite.

While Saints' razor-sharp attacking game had come to the fore against Saracens the previous weekend, this time they had to demonstrate their defensive resilience to defeat a London Irish side who had cut them to ribbons at the Madejski Stadium little more than a year earlier.

This was a more composed, resilient Northampton team than the one humbled 39-17 in Reading in October 2012, as Mallinder's men again showed how they had matured.

Backed by a typically sparse home crowd and the irksome pirate-sounding PA announcer, Irish threatened to cause more problems for Saints, but they weathered the storm and ensured Wilson's try and Myler's assured boot won out.

Myler's form had been nothing short of superb during the formative stages of the season as he shouldered the weight of being given sole possession of the Northampton No.10 shirt with aplomb.

He had been metronomic heading into this game and his kicking ability from the tee was crucial in deflating a home side buoyed by the presence of Australia star James O'Connor and, of course, the memories of that victory against Saints in the previous meeting at the Madejski.

There was relief in the visiting camp after the match as they knew they had scraped through another tricky assignment, once again exhibiting their character and team spirit.

'In the second half defensively we were very good,' Mallinder had said during his press conference in the clean-cut interview room. 'O'Connor came in for them and he played really well.

'They got the ball wide and they tested us in a lot of situations, but defensively we remained strong, which was pleasing.

'We didn't play to our best. We never reached the heights of last week but we got there in the end and when you're away from home that's important.'

Indeed, Saints kept ticking off the away games in the league and, the late agony at Gloucester aside, they were coming through largely unscathed, refusing to be beaten.

They were given a chance to take stock of a strong start in the Premiership and Heineken Cup as the glitz and glamour faded into the background to make way for the less attractive LV= Cup.

If Europe's premier club rugby competition and England's top division was like dining in Michelin-starred restaurants, playing in the LV= Cup was akin to eating at a greasy spoon, but there was still an appetite for it at Franklin's Gardens, especially among the young players, who were desperate to stake their claim for first-team action.

The upcoming games, at home to Gloucester and away to London Irish, would also give Mallinder an opportunity to rest and rotate, keeping his squad fresh for the return to Premiership action later in the month.

However, the director of rugby still wanted his team to maintain their momentum and there was a responsibility on the fringe players to continue the winning habit the club had managed to build up.

The incentive was certainly there, and the sight of Gloucester rocking up at the Gardens added more fuel to the fire, with the Cherry and Whites one of only two teams to have beaten Saints during the campaign.

Northampton were to get one up on the club from Kingsholm in the week leading up to the game as the Wanderers cruised past the Gloucester second string 49-9 on a comfortable Monday night at the Gardens.

Paul Diggin, Ethan Waller, Harrison, Packman, James Craig and Vasily Artemyev, who scored twice, secured a resounding success for Saints' shadow squad and Kiwi kicker Glenn Dickson added 14 points with the boot to put a gloss on the scoreline.

Many of those men would hope to play their part in the LV= Cup opener, with sights firmly set on stepping up the fight on all fronts and going all the way to the final, which would be held at Sandy Park, the home of the Exeter Chiefs, in March.

Game ten: Saturday, 9 November 2013: Northampton Saints 33 Gloucester 6 (LV= Cup group stage – game one)

Saints: Wilson; K Pisi, Stephenson, Waldouck, Packman (Artemyev 60); G Dickson (Olver 70), Glynn (A Day 52); A Waller (E Waller 56), Haywood (McMillan 65), Mercey (Denman 56), Verbakel, Craig (Woolford 65), Nutley, Harrison, van Velze.

Gloucester: M Thomas (L Evans 70); Sharples, Thorley, Tindall, Reynolds; F Burns (B Burns 72), Knoyle (Boughton 72); Gibbons (Y Thomas 45), George (Britton 50), Knight, James, Hicks, Cox, Kvesic (Hill 65), G Evans (Moriarty 55).

Referee: Steve Lee

Attendance: 12,870

Tries: Saints: Ken Pisi (2), Alex Day (2)

Conversions: Saints: Glenn Dickson, Sam Olver

Penalties: Saints: Glenn Dickson (3). **Gloucester:** Freddie Burns (2)

There may have been a different cast list, but it was a very familiar Saints show on Saturday. The 33-6 thrashing of Gloucester made it five games, five wins, four bonus points and 23 tries for Northampton at Franklin's Gardens this season.

Players may rotate in and out, but whatever the men in green, black and gold touch turns to, well ... gold.

There is a rich belief currently filtering through the club, with everyone from the tea lady to the chairman left with a warm feeling on departure from the Gardens.

It is a result of the squad Jim Mallinder has assembled and the hard work that has been done behind the scenes.

The club's Academy system is bearing fruit, as illustrated by Saturday's showing.

Mallinder pinpointed the likes of Alex Waller, Mike Haywood and Ben Nutley in his programme column, but was keen to stress there are many more where they came from.

The performances of players such as wing Howard Packman and scrum half Alex Day, both excellent on debut, suggest as much.

They are not quite as far down the track as the likes of Waller, who celebrated his 100th Saints appearance with the man of the match Champagne, or the tenacious Nutley.

But they are well on their way, you can be sure about that.

All in all, there is a good, balanced feel about the Saints squad.

Stellar names such as George North and Kahn Fotuali'i have arrived and passed on their wisdom to youngsters like Packman and Day.

Alex Corbisiero also made his way to the Gardens during the summer and it is clear his work with Waller is benefiting both parties.

There is a real band of brothers feel to the squad, with everyone backing each other up.

Messages fly between international stars and Academy graduates on social networking sites before games – and it's not just an act.

Skipper Dylan Hartley even sent a personal message to the Saints squad in the build-up to the Gloucester battle, telling the youngsters 'we owe them one'.

It is a sign of just how much camaraderie there is between the men dubbing themselves the 'Mo Bros' this November, as Hartley's Movember campaign gathers pace.

That is all for a good cause, and its knock-on effect is the galvanising of an already tight-knit Saints squad.

That is why the Wanderers are gunning for A League glory, having finished top of their pool, outscoring every other team.

They are not Saints' second team. They are just Saints.

And that is why Saturday's performance was so seamless.

A good start in the Premiership, a good start in the Champions Cup and now a good start in the LV= Cup. No wonder Saints attack coach Alex King was beaming after this display as he poured praise on a team determined to do the treble.

'It's important for this club that we fight on all three fronts,' King said as he reflected on another impressive team performance. 'I'm delighted we got the bonus point against Gloucester. I thought all the subs did well when they came on.

'We were thoroughly professional and it was a good Gloucester team we were playing.

'I've got high hopes for all of our young players.'

Scrum half Alex Day was the young player who stole the spotlight with two tries on his Saints debut, but there were plenty of other reasons for the coaches to be positive, with others such as Stephenson and Packman giving glimpses into the future.

Saints may have made 11 changes to the team that won at London Irish on the previous weekend, but this was no weakened team and the fans at Franklin's Gardens were treated to an entertaining display.

Mallinder had masterminded another winning formula, blending the likes of Dom Waldouck, who was captain for the day, and Alex Waller, who was making his 100th appearance for the club, with fresh-faced youngsters revelling in running out in front of a close-to-full Franklin's Gardens.

It was a potent mix and Saints' team selection worked far better than Gloucester's as the away side's 12 alterations resulted in a disjointed performance.

Freddie Burns did get a couple of penalties on the board for the men in a pink and blue kit that was as uninspiring as their performance. Gloucester showed that they didn't have the same depth as their opponents, who could harbour realistic hopes of making that Sandy Park showpiece.

They would soon have another hurdle to overcome, with another LV= Cup game, at London Irish, on the following weekend, but it was clear that everyone in the squad had taken real confidence from the win against Gloucester.

Day took time to reflect on a 'really special' first Saints appearance, while centurion Waller had reasons of his own to celebrate.

'It was fantastic to make the 100 with the boys and get the win,' said the Kettering-born front row forward. 'It was a really proud moment for me and I'm just glad I could share it with all the lads.

'There are a lot of young lads who hadn't played before, who were making their debuts, and they really stepped up.

'You look at players like Sam Olver and they really showed they could hold their own, so it only bodes well for the future of the club.'

So impressive was the whole Saints squad that praise was even starting to come their way from up the motorway. Leicester legend Lewis Moody was tipping this to be Northampton's year, feeling confident that his old rivals would add some welcome silverware to the cabinet at the Gardens.

When those of a Tigers persuasion show you respect, you know you must be doing something right, and Saints looked to continue on their upward curve at the Madejski Stadium.

However, in the lead-up to the second LV= Cup game of the season, there was to be plenty of bad news. It is said things often come in threes, and that was the case as, first, Corbisiero suffered another injury blow.

The prop, who had come off the bench to play 39 minutes in England's 31-12 win against Argentina on the same day as Saints beat Gloucester, was due to start against New Zealand at the weekend, but he was forced to withdraw after picking up a training injury and would need surgery on his knee.

Just after that news emerged, more problems were to come from another international camp as George Pisi was banned for six weeks for a tip tackle executed on Tommy Bowe during Samoa's defeat to Ireland in Dublin on the previous weekend.

That would rule Pisi out of the crucial Heineken Cup double-header against Leinster in December and it was a sizeable disappointment for Saints as they would have to tinker with a midfield partnership – between Pisi and Burrell – that had served them so well. To top it all off, Craig, who had been as unlucky with injuries as Corbisiero, would go under the knife to rectify a shoulder problem, meaning three men were added to the absences list within the space of just a few days.

Nevertheless, Saints marched into the Madejski on the back of four successive wins, with injury worries far from the forefront of their minds as they sought to claim a second win in Berkshire in the space of just three weeks.

A day after five of their senior stars just failed to help England beat the All Blacks at Twickenham – Hartley, on his 50th appearance for his country, Lawes, Wood, Lee Dickson and Foden were all among the starting 15 for the 30-22 defeat – Saints' other squad members would get another chance to fire on a Sunday afternoon at the home of Irish.

It might be a fixture far from the glamour of a game against New Zealand, but the players who boarded the bus to Reading knew that if they could make it two wins from as many games in the Anglo-Welsh competition, they would take another giant leap towards the semi-finals.

For some, it was also one more chance to stake their claim for inclusion in the first-team squad for the return to league action a week later. Make no mistake, there was more than just points to play for.

Game 11: Sunday, 17 November 2013: London Irish 18 Northampton Saints 39 (LV= Cup group stage – game two)

London Irish: Lewington; Fowlie, Armitage, Sa, Fenby; Dorrian, Allinson (Mulchrone 76); Parr (Harris 66), Mayhew (Stevens 76), Hagan (Halavatau 40), A Toolis, B Toolis, Danaher (c) (Kenny 39), Evans, Low (Lonergan 76).

Saints: Wilson (Olver 66); Packman (Skelcey 78), Stephenson, Waldouck (c), Collins; G Dickson, A Day (Glynn 60); E Waller (Denman 66), McMillan (Williams 66), Ma'afu (Mercey 57), Verbakel, C Day (Woolford 66), Nutley, Harrison (Clark 62), van Velze.

Referee: Rhys Thomas

Attendance: 5,792

Tries: London Irish: Danny Kenny, Kieran Low. **Saints:** Howard Packman, Ethan Waller, Ben Nutley

Conversions: London Irish: Myles Dorrian. **Saints:** Glenn Dickson (3)

Penalties: London Irish: Myles Dorrian (2). **Saints:** Glenn Dickson (6)

There are 36 player profiles in the first team section on the Saints website – yet 20 of those men were missing at the Madejski Stadium on Sunday.

The likes of Dylan Hartley and Tom Wood starred for England on Saturday, George North scored for Wales, Kahn Fotuali'i registered for Samoa and others, like Stephen Myler and Luther Burrell, were rested.

No matter, Jim Mallinder simply made use of the men who were left, blending them with a number of Senior Academy stars to conjure up a potent mix that left London Irish reeling.

Saints dished out a Berkshire battering, surging to a 39-18 LV= Cup win, their fifth successive victory in all competitions.

It was a comprehensive triumph full of purpose and panache, two qualities in short supply in the Irish camp.

And it was another showcase of the immense talent pool now at Mallinder's disposal as many of the players who were part of the 33-6 win against Gloucester eight days earlier impressed again.

One of them, young wing Howard Packman, got his first senior try, showing good awareness and great speed to put the finishing touches to a fine breakaway score.

Ethan Waller continued on his steep upward curve, proving a menace in the tight and the loose as he also scored for the first time in the Saints first team.

Glenn Dickson, one of the more senior members of the side at 27, booted 24 points, missing just one of his ten kicks from the tee and controlling the game well.

But the star of the show was Ben Nutley, who produced his finest display in Saints colours, setting up Packman for the first try and writing his own name on the scoresheet late on.

Nutley was superb in attack and defence and has used pre-season, during which he was a stand-out figure, and the LV= Cup to stake his claim.

He will surely get more game time in the coming weeks as he looks to push the likes of Phil Dowson and Calum Clark all the way for a starting spot.

It appears to be his time and if Sunday's showing is anything to go by, Northampton have got plenty to look forward to from the former Luton Town youth team goalkeeper.

He is a glowing example of the grit and determination currently swelling the Saints squad, which almost appears to have three tiers.

Even players like Alex Waller and Mike Haywood, men learning their trade and providing good back-up for Alex Corbisiero and Hartley, were given the week off.

But their deputies, Ethan Waller and Ross McMillan, stepped in and excelled.

Put simply, there is an incredible depth to this Northampton group.

The LV= Cup team was asked to maintain the momentum gathered by wins against Ospreys, Saracens and Irish, and they've more than done that.

The 72 points scored is a demonstration of the success during the past two weeks.

Some international stars return for the game against Newcastle Falcons this week, and now it's their turn to keep the pace.

By the end of this match, the well of superlatives was running dry, as Saints' squad continued to stand up to the strain – and in style.

London Irish provided another example of a group of players who simply could not match the amount of quality they found themselves up against and though there were very few first-team players involved for Saints once again, it mattered not.

Men such as classy flanker Nutley and loosehead prop Ethan Waller seized their opportunities with big, try-scoring displays, ensuring their club would win at the Madejski Stadium for the second time during the calendar month.

However, whereas the Premiership meeting two weeks earlier was a rather cagey affair, this was an open encounter, with plenty of attacking rugby, iced by Waller capping his first Saints start with a try.

Glenn Dickson continually kicked Irish where it hurt, landing a massive nine efforts from the tee, and the final scoreline was a glossy one for a group of players who had given their coaches some welcome selection dilemmas ahead of the following week's league game at home to Newcastle Falcons.

The only disappointment had been the failure to secure the try bonus point, but Saints were motoring towards the semi-finals with just two more group games, against Newport Gwent Dragons and Saracens, to come in January and February.

For now though, all eyes were on that Falcons clash at Franklin's Gardens, and Mallinder's door was certain to get a few knocks during the week, with plenty of players desperate to keep their place and others eager to get back into the team.

'I've been pleased with how many players have come in and performed well over the past four weeks, both in the Aviva Premiership and LV= Cup,' Mallinder said.

'We've had eight debutants in all and the squad have built a good amount of momentum with four wins on top of the Ospreys victory back in October.

'We've played well on the whole and several players have staked a claim for continued inclusion. It makes our selections as coaches that bit more difficult.

'The England boys produced some outstanding performances over the three Tests at Twickenham but they are by no means certain to go straight back into the starting 15 this weekend.'

Mallinder's selection headache eased slightly due to injuries to Hartley and Wood, who were rendered unavailable for the Newcastle clash, while Fotuali'i, Ken Pisi, North and Artemyev still had international commitments to deal with.

Manoa, who had been named Premiership player of the month for October thanks to barnstorming displays against Leicester and Saracens, was also still absent as he represented the USA, while Corbisiero and Craig were still injured and George Pisi suspended.

Mallinder still had the likes of Lawes, Lee Dickson and Foden heading back from the England camp, while a plethora of stars, who had been rested during the LV= Cup weeks, were back in the frame. But what would the director of rugby do, and would it work against a Falcons team they were fully expected to flay at Franklin's Gardens?

Game 12: Saturday, 23 November 2013: Northampton Saints 18 Newcastle Falcons 0 (Aviva Premiership – round eight)

Saints: Foden (Waldouck 61); Elliott, Wilson (G Dickson 73), Burrell, Collins; Myler, Dickson (A Day 73); A Waller (E Waller 65), Haywood (McMillan 73), Ma'afu, Lawes (Nutley 65), Day (van Velze 64), Clark, Dowson (c), Dickinson.

Newcastle Falcons: Tait; Cato, Barnes, Powell (York 68), Shortland; Godman (Clegg 65), Blair (Fury 65); Vickers, Lawson, Tomaszczyk (Wilson 63), del Fava, McKenzie (MacLeod 59), Mayhew, Welch (c), Hogg (Fitzpatrick 68).

Referee: Dean Richards

Attendance: 12,415

Tries: Saints: James Wilson, Luther Burrell

Conversions: Saints: Stephen Myler

Penalties: Saints: Stephen Myler (2)

Not playing to your full potential and winning is said to be the hallmark of champions.

So if you don't play to your full potential but win and also keep a clean sheet you must be doing something right.

That was the case for Saints on Saturday as they produced a far from vintage display against Newcastle.

But, despite a lack of fluency, partly inflicted on themselves, partly due to the Falcons' dogged nature, they claimed victory and completely shut the opposition out.

Dean Richards' men, as demonstrated by the fact they had won three of their seven league games prior to this one, are no mugs. They are a team fighting for Premiership survival, which gets closer every week thanks to Worcester's continual struggle.

We'll come back to that later.

When you are a team like Saints, expected to challenge for the title, teams don't come to your place and lie down.

They scrap for every inch, desperate to spring a surprise that would dominate the rugby section of the Sunday papers.

Newcastle never looked likely to hog the headlines, but they did ensure Saints had to work hard for their recognition.

Richards has instilled a steely determination in his side and some of their defending was hugely impressive.

Ryan Shortland set the tone with an early try-saving tackle on Tom Collins and that rearguard action continued until the 58th minute, when James Wilson finally broke through.

Saints had unusually stuttered in their build-up play until a fine gather and break from Jamie Elliott teed up intelligent centre Wilson.

It was the key to the door and Luther Burrell added a second try soon after to make sure there would be no smash and grab.

The Falcons never really looked likely to claim anything from the game, but they showed no lack of belief and refused to crumble. That is to their credit, and it was a good test for Saints – though the players and coaches refused to label it a wake-up call – ahead of the game at Worcester on Saturday.

That match is less banana skin, more oil slick for Jim Mallinder's men and patience may be required to pick up the points from Sixways. Like Newcastle, the Warriors will be desperate for a Saints-sized scalp and will not roll over easily.

So, in that respect, Saturday's game was perfect preparation.

What was important was that there was no upset – that four points were picked up and the winning run, which has now stretched to six games, was maintained.

Saints still sit second in the Aviva Premiership and if they keep picking up wins in whatever fashion necessary they won't be too far off where they want to be.

In the build-up to this game, Wilson was discussing Saints' new simplistic style.

'We're not looking to light up the world with this amazing game of rugby,' said the Kiwi utility back. 'It's simple rugby we're playing but we're playing it really well and that's key. It's what we want to keep on doing.

'We're putting pressure on teams and making them play a bit. It's simple stuff done really well and that's helping us out.'

And how those words rang true in this encounter. Saints certainly didn't light up the world with their rugby. In truth, this was a game to get through and get out of with as many points as possible.

Newcastle Falcons came to frustrate, employing a tactic known in football as *catenaccio* – which is the Italian word for 'door bolt' – to see if they could nick something with limited possession, which made for a far from entertaining encounter.

Saints had scored 23 tries in five previous home games and they huffed and puffed until they eventually blew the door down through Wilson and Burrell, who was back in the team having not had the England action he had desired during the autumn internationals.

Mallinder had brought Lawes, Lee Dickson and Foden back into the team and their experience was useful after a first half that failed to yield a try. Saints didn't panic and they got the job done, meaning they had stretched their winning run to six games in all competitions.

'We won 18-0, we stopped them from scoring, we'd have loved to have gone on and scored four tries but sometimes that doesn't happen and we won the game,' said Mallinder, who was sporting a strong moustache in aid of the club's Movember campaign.

'We needed to take our opportunities. We weren't quite as cohesive as we have been this season.'

Nevertheless, the fact Saints had maintained their momentum and their winning streak was all that mattered ahead of the final Premiership game before the two huge Heineken Cup clashes with Leinster.

The only real issue came in the form of Foden, with the full back having limped off in the 61st minute with a knee injury. Mallinder was optimistic, but there was no doubt it was a worry, with more testing encounters ahead in the next month or so.

Saints, now second in the Premiership table, would see the pressure ramped up during the period that followed, starting with the trip to winless Worcester Warriors.

Wilson was on media duty again after the Falcons game, already setting his sights on the Warriors, who he knew would be relishing the chance to end their own barren run by beating a side at the other end of the form table.

Clark also issued a warning, stressing that the Warriors were a 'proud bunch of lads' and adding 'all they need is a win and we don't want to be the team they get it against'.

Saints would have to go to Sixways without Foden as his scan two days after the Newcastle game showed that he had suffered PCL (posterior cruciate ligament) damage, ruling him out for three months.

It was a massive blow for Mallinder's men and the director of rugby quickly made a point of praising Waldouck, who, with George Pisi still banned, would be an option to come in at centre, with Wilson switching to full back.

However, Wilson was also ruled out for the game at Worcester, opening the door for Glenn Dickson, with the fly half facing a baptism of fire as he was thrown in at full back on his first Premiership start.

Waldouck did come in at centre, while there was plenty of positive injury news as Wood, Hartley and Manoa all returned to the team as Saints sought to avoid a shock defeat at Sixways.

Game 13: Saturday, 30 November 2013: Worcester Warriors 10 Northampton Saints 33 (Aviva Premiership – round nine)

Worcester: Pennell; Stephenson, Grove, Matavesi, Hammond; Mieres, Hodgson (Su'a 44); Fainga'anuku, Brooker (Shervington 50), O'Donnell (Andress 58), Percival, Galarza, de Carpentier, Betty, Thomas (c).

Saints: G Dickson (Artemyev 76); K Pisi, Waldouck, Burrell (Stephenson 73), Collins; Myler, L Dickson; A Waller (E Waller 67), Hartley (c) (Haywood 72), Ma'afu (Mercey 52), Manoa, Day (Lawes 52), Clark (Dowson 52), Wood, Dickinson.

Referee: Tim Wigglesworth

Attendance: 7,808

Tries: Worcester: Ignacio Mieres. **Saints:** Samu Manoa, Tom Collins, Tom Wood

Conversions: Worcester: Ignacio Mieres. **Saints:** Stephen Myler (3)

Penalties: Worcester: Chris Pennell. **Saints:** Stephen Myler (4)

A sizeable Saints support headed to Sixways more in expectation than hope on Saturday.

Many members of the green, black and gold fraternity would have been expecting a comfortable success, garnished with a glut of tries.

Worcester, after all, had lost all eight of their Premiership games, shipping 224 points in the process.

But this wasn't to be as straightforward as some fans and pundits had predicted and the players and management had hoped.

As the game hit the 60-minute mark, everyone of a Saints persuasion was preparing themselves for a sharp shock.

Worcester had blunted the opposition threat, leading 10-9 thanks to Ignacio Mieres' try and conversion and a penalty from full back Chris Pennell.

But they just couldn't hold on, eventually being overawed by the strength of the Saints bench.

Tom Mercey, Courtney Lawes and Phil Dowson were among the cavalry called for to change the game – and they succeeded.

Anyone who has played team sport will have empathised with Worcester.

You work so hard for three-quarters of the game, belying your underdog status, only to see fresh, talented players emerge from the opposition bench.

It feels like you're back to square one, having to start again to stem a threat that refuses to go away.

And, eventually, the inevitable happens: you crumble and the floodgates open.

Once Samu Manoa had broken the resistance on 63 minutes, it was no surprise that Saints started to flow.

Tom Collins grabbed his first senior try as Worcester found themselves exposed out wide before Tom Wood eased over the line, teed up by Premiership debutant Tom Stephenson.

Suddenly, with six minutes to go, a Saints team lacking in ideas for much of the match had their sights set on the bonus point.

It's the crazy nature of the game we follow – and it isn't half interesting.

Much has been made of the fact Saints only took eight points from a possible ten against strugglers Newcastle and Worcester.

But if you could look at the fixture list before the season, predict what would happen and see it unfold, it wouldn't be sport. It would be boring, predictable.

That the Falcons and the Warriors toughed it out and refused to give in is a sign of how intriguing the Premiership is.

They wanted a Saints-shaped scalp and though they didn't get it, it is to their credit that they made a title-chasing team battle all the way.

For Jim Mallinder's men, all that mattered was winning, especially with the plethora of personnel they had missing.

Ben Foden, George Pisi, James Wilson, Kahn Fotuali'i and George North all have the skills to unlock a team like Worcester, but none of those stellar names were present.

Instead, players such as Dom Waldouck and Glenn Dickson were thrown in for first Premiership starts of the season and Academy graduate Collins was on the wing again.

It is not easy to develop a rhythm in the back line when you are constantly having to chop and change.

It takes time to build up partnerships and mutual understanding. That showed on Saturday, as Saints struggled to get into the groove. But, as was mentioned last week, the sign of a good team is the ability to adapt to different circumstances and to win when you're not playing well.

That was exactly what Saints did – and once again they sent their fans home happy, rather than with a big upset to chew over.

For a long period at Sixways, Saints supporters were rubbing their eyes in disbelief, genuinely fearing that the worst was going to happen.

Worcester had belied their winless status to put real pressure on Mallinder's men, who were struggling to break down a stubborn side with one of the biggest upsets in Premiership history in their sights.

Prior to the game, there had been plenty of trepidation among the home fans, who could have been forgiven for fearing another disappointing day at the stadium, despite the relentless optimism of the Sixways PA announcer.

However, as the game went on, there was more of a buzz around the place, with belief growing that this could be the day that Worcester won their first game of the season and the day that Saints' march was halted in shuddering fashion.

That belief was eventually crushed as Saints brought on some real power from the bench and the Warriors' fight faded. It was no real surprise because, as is so often the case for struggling sides, clearing the final hurdle in a game to get the win is the hardest part.

Saints kept their nerve, stayed just a point behind and eventually pulled clear in the closing stages, showing their class and their strong mentality, which was making them a real contender for silverware.

The likes of Wood, a former Worcester player, and Manoa were Saints' warriors, upping the physicality levels and bringing down the mood among those previously buoyant home supporters.

While Mallinder, still with that magnificent Movember moustache, was left to salute his side's super-subs, including Lawes, who was labelled 'outstanding', Worcester director of rugby Dean Ryan was ruing his team's inability to convert a winning position.

'For 60 minutes we were very competitive, but not competitive in the last 10 or 15,' Ryan said. 'When they roll the kind of people they did off the bench it's an indication of the depth they've got.'

Ryan was later asked whether he truly believed his side would win the game when they were 10-9 up with just 20 minutes to go.

'No, not really,' he replied, before going on to express his disappointment with how referees seemed to favour the Premiership's 'powerhouse sides' in the key moments in matches.

That didn't matter to Saints though. They had got what they came for and were just happy to head home unscathed, with four more precious points added to their Premiership tally.

They now had far bigger fish to fry, with those two huge matches against Leinster looming large on the horizon. The

Irish giants would be heading to Franklin's Gardens just six days after the win at Sixways and Saints knew they had to be at 100 per cent if they were to keep their Heineken Cup flame burning.

North and Corbisiero received a boost ahead of the game as the Lions stars were named in the IRPA Players' World XV of the Year, alongside the likes of Kieran Read and Leigh Halfpenny.

However, for North, what mattered most was the events to come in the next two weeks, with the Welsh behemoth knowing what was at stake for him and his Saints team-mates.

The 2014 Heineken Cup Final was to be held in Cardiff, prompting North to dream of a magnificent homecoming, but he knew exactly how difficult it would be to realise that fantasy, especially with Leinster providing an immediate barrier.

'It would be really nice to come home to Cardiff for the Heineken Cup Final in May, but we have two very difficult games against Leinster to overcome before we can start thinking about that,' North had said.

Meanwhile, Ken Pisi was also looking no further than Leinster, and one man in particular. The Samoan conducted one of the happiest pre-match interviews of the season, expressing his excitement at facing his childhood hero, Brian O'Driscoll.

'It's my first time playing against O'Driscoll,' Pisi said, donning that trademark smile.

'When I was young, I was watching him on television and pretending I was him. It will be really good to finally play against him. I admired his skill and everything about his game. He's been one to watch. He's awesome and hopefully I'll get to play against him and beat him as well.'

Those sentiments were certainly echoed by the rest of the Saints camp as they headed into the biggest game of their season so far.

King spoke about the match being a barometer, showing his club exactly where they stood in a season in which they had shown they were capable of competing with and beating the best England had to offer. He knew battling Leinster would be another step up though because the Dublin-based outfit had won three of the previous five Heineken Cup competitions, including in 2011 when they poured so much pain on Saints with a 33-22 victory in the Cardiff showpiece.

This fixture was a chance to put those demons to bed and to show Leinster that Northampton meant business ahead of the following week's renewal of rivalries at the Aviva Stadium.

The Saints went marching in at the Gardens on the back of seven successive wins, and confidence was high as they sought a victory that would easily eclipse any of those that had gone before.

Game 14: Saturday, 7 December 2013: Northampton Saints 7 Leinster 40 (Heineken Cup pool stages – game three)

Saints: K Pisi; Elliott (Collins 72), Waldouck, Burrell, North; Myler (G Dickson 68), L Dickson (Glynn 68); A Waller (E Waller 58), Hartley (c) (Haywood 58), Mercey (Denman 60), Manoa, Lawes, Wood, Dowson (Clark 58), Dickinson (C Day 40).

Leinster: R Kearney; D Kearney (Kirchner 54), O'Driscoll (Gopperth 71), D'Arcy, Fitzgerald; Madigan, Reddan (Cooney 64); McGrath (Bent 64), Cronin (Dundon 68), Ross (Moore 68), Toner, McCarthy (Cullen 60), Ruddock, O'Brien (Jennings 32), Heaslip (c).

Referee: Nigel Owens

Attendance: 13,475

Tries: Saints: Lee Dickson. **Leinster:** Luke Fitzgerald (3), Jamie Heaslip, Eoin Reddan, Brian O'Driscoll

Conversions: Saints: Stephen Myler. **Leinster:** Ian Madigan (5)

You could say it was the stuff of nightmares – but what happened at Franklin's Gardens on Saturday evening may even have been beyond Saints supporters' wildest hallucinations.

Six tries conceded, one scored. Leinster played rugby from a different planet to bring Northampton, who had won their previous seven games, crashing down to earth.

It was a savage reality check for Jim Mallinder's men.

They hadn't played to their full potential in recent wins against Newcastle and Worcester, but still prevailed.

This, though, was a different challenge altogether. A below-par performance against Leinster will be punished. And so it was. In crushing fashion.

Saints got a taste of their own medicine.

They had done to them what they have inflicted on plenty of others this season.

Leinster, as acknowledged by all fair-minded fans at the Gardens, were far too good. They were unrelenting and ruthless.

Saints were caught cold and couldn't get into the stride that has served them so well this season.

It was reminiscent of last December, when Ulster came to town and did a 25-6 demolition job.

This was worse than that, though. An evisceration of the sort Leicester dished out at the Gardens in March.

The common denominator? Matt O'Connor, the Leinster boss and former Tigers coach.

His smile in the press room after the game said it all. Two visits to Northampton in 2013. A 76-15 personal aggregate win.

As for the Saints representatives put in the firing line after the game; Tom Wood and Jim Mallinder were refreshing.

There was no hiding place – and they didn't seek one.

They gave a brutally honest assessment of what they had just witnessed, struggling to find positives.

One is that Saints have been here before. That Ulster defeat last December was followed by a defiant display in Belfast, resulting in a brilliant 10-9 win.

Whether Saints can do that this time remains to be seen.

They are currently blighted by injuries to key men, a story told by the sight of Alex Corbisiero and Ben Foden suited and booted on the pitch at half-time.

Corbisiero, who is out for between three to four months with a knee injury, was on crutches; Foden, out for a similar spell, in a surgical boot.

The first-half performance was that bad, you almost wanted to put them on at the break to see what they could do.

How Saints could have done with them fully fit and at their best. Big-name players are required when the big games come around. Kahn Fotuali'i, James Wilson and George Pisi were also unavailable. How they were missed.

A last-minute reshuffle, sparked by Wilson's post-warm-up withdrawal, pushed Ken Pisi to full back, which is not a position he is used to. It didn't work, and Leinster took advantage.

Pisi had highlighted Brian O'Driscoll as his childhood hero in the build-up to the game, and the Ireland legend showed why he is so revered with a sensational all-round display.

Pisi's dreams of facing his idol were to turn into harsh reality.

For Saints there was a similar grounding effect.

The win they had fantasised about got further away with every passing second.

Now they will have to dream big if they are to believe they can repeat last year's Ravenhill rally at the Aviva Stadium next Saturday.

'Embarrassed' was how Mallinder summed up his feelings after this one.

'Like an uncontested team run' was Wood's take on it.

The faces of both men told the story as they struggled to comprehend what they had just been part of.

A seven-match winning streak was crushed in the most savage fashion as the blue flags of Leinster's supporters were waved all around a ground awash with Irishmen basking in the sheer brilliance of their team's ruthless display.

At times, Saints supporters just wanted to shout 'stop, stop, we're already dead', but Leinster just kept coming and there was no answer given as salt continued to be rubbed in the painful wound.

In a season that already had so many peaks, this was a real trough and Saints had seen that Heineken Cup flame all but extinguished before the break as the away side scored four times. There was no let-up in the second period either, as Leinster piled more misery on their hosts.

Saints did at least grab a consolation try, from Lee Dickson, but there was a real fear that they were now in the middle of two weeks that would damage their confidence so much that it could have a sizeable knock-on effect.

The following week's fixture in Dublin needed to at least provide a shot in the arm, a morale boost for the weeks and months to come. All the right things were said in the aftermath of the gargantuan Gardens defeat. Lee Dickson said he was 'sure' the players would deliver in Dublin, Wood spoke about 'showing the real Northampton' and Mallinder told his men not to let the humbling defeat define them.

Saints had turned the tables on Ulster just a year earlier, when, having been hammered at the Gardens, they bounced back in Belfast, claiming a stunning 10-9 victory against all the odds.

The spirit displayed in that Ravenhill success was striking and though many supporters doubted that history could repeat itself, it was at least there, in the memory, to call upon in what promised to be a tough week leading up to the return against Leinster.

Mallinder and his coaching staff had a huge job to pick the players up, but the determination among the group was palpable and as the week went on, everyone of a Northampton persuasion at least dared to dream about what could unfold.

Whatever happened, the supporters would make the most of the trip to the city, but how sweet it would be if they could sink some Guinness knowing their team had restored pride.

However, putting a plaster on the wounds was the least Saints wanted to do. They wanted to do what they had done to Ulster. To win in their backyard and make them feel some of the pain they had felt at the Gardens.

Mallinder called on his players to use the trip to Dublin as a springboard for the weeks and months ahead, telling them that Leinster had shown them the level they needed to now reach.

Little did Mallinder, the players and supporters know that those words would be followed to the letter, and what was to happen in Dublin would be a realisation of the club's wildest dreams.

Game 15: Saturday, 14 December 2013: Leinster 9 Northampton Saints 18 (Heineken Cup pool stages – game four)

Leinster: R Kearney; D Kearney (Kirchner 60), O'Driscoll, D'Arcy (Gopperth 79), Fitzgerald; Madigan, Reddan; McGrath (Bent 57), Cronin, Ross (Moore 60), Toner, McCarthy (Cullen 73), Ruddock (McLaughlin 57), Jennings, Heaslip (c).

Saints: K Pisi; Elliott, North, Burrell, Collins; Myler, L Dickson (Fotuali'i 53); A Waller (E Waller 70), Hartley (c) (Haywood 73), Ma'afu (Mercey 53), Lawes (Dowson 73), Day, Clark, Wood, Manoa (Dickinson 67).

Referee: Jerome Garces

Attendance: 47,370

Tries: Saints: George North, Jamie Elliott

Conversions: Saints: Stephen Myler

Penalties: Leinster: Ian Madigan (3). **Saints:** Stephen Myler

Drop goals: Saints: Kahn Fotuali'i

There have been some heroic showings in the recent history of Northampton Saints, but perhaps none more so than the one they produced in Dublin on Saturday night.

This, after all, was a Saints team that had been embarrassed by Leinster a week earlier. The 40-7 defeat at Franklin's Gardens was an evisceration. An utter annihilation.

But only when you have reached your nadir can you truly appreciate the highest of highs – and that was the case for Northampton at the Aviva Stadium.

The outpouring of emotion as Jamie Elliott burst towards the Leinster line after the clock had gone dead was immense.

Saints fans everywhere, at the ground and at home, roared the diminutive winger on and even press box professionalism went out of the window.

Because this was a moment for everyone of a Northampton persuasion to savour.

A memory to endure the harshest of Temple Bar-inspired hangovers.

Saints fans will watch that final sequence of events over and over again, pinching themselves to make sure it wasn't all some sort of wild hallucination.

Leinster had looked sure to score as the 80-minute mark approached. Phase after phase went by as they set up camp on the Saints line.

It seemed like an eternity.

It felt like another Munster moment was beckoning, as victory looked like it would be ripped from the Northampton grasp in the cruellest of fashions.

But Saints, as they had for the entirety of the game, stood strong, their iron will on show as they refused to be punctured.

And when Jamie Heaslip spilled the ball, Elliott, sharp as a tack, picked it up and ran for his life, denying the Irish team even the consolation of a bonus point.

Passion and pride packaged in green, black and gold. The Saints boys weren't going to be beaten. Not again.

They were labelled embarrassing by some sections of the home support a week earlier. This time they were the antithesis.

Northampton were strong, determined and unbreakable.

To only concede nine points, via three Ian Madigan penalties, in the Aviva Stadium hothouse is an incredible effort.

It was reminiscent of Ravenhill last year. It had a hint of Allianz Park in May. But, really, this was incomparable to anything that had gone before.

Saints didn't win the Heineken Cup with this triumph. Heck, they face a struggle just to get out of the pool this season as they remain four points adrift of Leinster.

But whatever happens from here on in, they have given their town something to be proud of. It seems criminal that there may not be English representation in the Heineken Cup next season.

It will be a huge loss to the competition because battles like this Anglo-Irish ding-dong are what it's all about.

Excitement, exhilaration and true underdog spirit shining through. It was written before the game that Saints are at their best with their backs to the wall. They are dangerous when backed into a corner. And so it proved.

They have lost just four times away from home in 2013. A quite amazing record. The 'Why not us?' phrase may have had its day, but the meaning behind it lives on. And so will memories of this magical December night in Dublin.

It took some time to sum up what Saints had produced at the Aviva Stadium because it didn't seem like words could do their performance justice.

It was not just the display, but the context in which they produced it, having gone from humiliated and humbled to proud and unbreakable.

They pieced themselves back together to deliver a comeback that was the greatest since Lazarus, putting Leinster to the sword in front of their own fans and walking away with one of the most seismic wins in Heineken Cup history.

Pockets of Saints fans celebrated in the Aviva Stadium, struggling to believe what they had just witnessed from a team they thought were in for another hiding.

The coaches, who, while confident in their players, would have expected them to struggle to produce a victory, were jubilant, and the players mirrored those emotions.

In the post-match press conference, Mallinder and Hartley were, understandably, still trying to take it all in.

Mallinder, who tried to keep a lid on things by describing it as 'one of the good wins', issued a message to his players, telling them to soak up the experience of winning in Dublin by taking in the best bars the city had to offer.

'We'll enjoy tonight,' he said. 'I hope the lads go out, have a few beers and experience what Dublin's all about, especially on the back of a win. Last week it felt like being in Dublin, at home, and that really hurt, their supporters celebrating and that's a terrible feeling. We don't want that to happen again.'

It hadn't happened again, and the players certainly made the most of their boss giving them free rein to celebrate wildly. Many of them could be seen wandering down Harcourt Street, Dublin's main clubbing strip, in the early hours, as they, fans and Northampton-based journalists celebrated alike.

It was a night that deserved to be crowned with a proper party in a city that knows how to throw them. Hartley had admitted it had been a 'long week' after his side 'got beat up at home' – and this was the perfect way to end it.

However, when the hangovers eased and the plane returned to England, everyone at Saints knew there was plenty more work to be done.

The Dublin delight could make or break their season. They could live up to the expectation it brought, or they could let it crush them.

They knew they needed to ensure there was no case of after the Lord Mayor's show by keeping their league bid on track and there was the small matter of an Aviva A League Final to look forward to just two days after that momentous evening in Ireland.

Bath would provide the opposition in the second-team showpiece, with the Wanderers welcoming the West Country side to the Gardens, desperate to secure the first silverware of the season.

On the day of the game, it was announced that Russian wing Artemyev would be heading back to Russia and his appearance for the Wanderers would be his last in Northampton colours.

Meanwhile, on a busy afternoon of news, the arrival of American back row forward Cam Dolan was confirmed, with supporters hoping he could be the next USA sensation at Saints, following Manoa's relentless heroics.

Dolan had come in as injury cover for Craig and was described by Mallinder as a player with 'natural talent and the physical attributes it takes to succeed', but Saints supporters would have to wait to see him get some game time.

Firstly, the A League Final had to be negotiated and it was to be contested by two strong groups of players with the Wanderers, who had beaten Harlequins in the semi-finals, including Glenn Dickson, Stephenson, Ethan Waller and Haywood in their squad.

Those four players had been part of the squad that won at Leinster, but they were unable to enjoy similar success against

FROM SAINTS TO WINNERS

the Bath second string, who called on the likes of Gavin Henson and Nick Abendanon to help them take the trophy home from Northampton.

It was a gutsy showing from the Wanderers, but, having come back from 17-3 down to level at the break, they were eventually beaten 29-20, seeing their hopes of glory shattered.

There was to be some better news in the days that followed as Wood, Christian Day, Dickinson, Nutley and Haywood all signed new deals, and those men then turned their attentions to events on the following weekend.

Wasps were to provide the opposition on the return to league matters, and all of the talk was about showing Dai Young's men the same respect as had been afforded to Leinster in Dublin.

Saints knew winning at Adams Park would not be quite as tough as delivering at the Aviva Stadium, but, nevertheless, there was still a sizeable physical challenge to be negotiated, as well as making sure the mental side of the game functioned.

Hartley, Lawes and Lee Dickson were given a bit of a breather as they took their places on the bench but Haywood, Dickinson and Fotuali'i were far from bad replacements to have.

Collins kept his place, having come in at the last minute in the win at Leinster and produced a performance that belied his youth, but Foden, Corbisiero, Wilson, Waldouck, Craig and George Pisi were still on the missing list.

Having completed the remarkable turnaround at Ulster a year earlier, Saints then lost their next game, seeing Harlequins defeat them on a disappointing day at the Gardens, so they were desperate not to let a big win be followed by an irksome loss on this occasion.

Sitting second in the Premiership standings ahead of the trip to High Wycombe, they would engage in a pivotal round of Premiership action, which included Saracens facing Leicester and Bath hosting Harlequins.

It meant that Mallinder's men knew they had every chance of claiming the Christmas No.1 spot if they could win at Wasps and that sharpened the focus further ahead of a trip to a ground where the Tigers had already been tamed during the campaign.

Could Saints keep the fizz of that Dublin night alive or would they fall flat against the league's seventh-placed side? They desperately wanted the former to be true, but it wouldn't be easy to keep the feel-good vibes flowing.

Game 16: Saturday, 21 December 2013: Wasps 15 Northampton Saints 17 (Aviva Premiership – round ten)

Wasps: Daly; Helu, Bell (c), Hayter, Varndell; Goode (Carlisle 44), Davies (Simpson 62); Mullan, Festuccia (Lindsay 62), Cooper-Woolley (Swainston 64), Palmer, Launchbury, Johnson, Haskell (Thompson 65), Jones.

Saints: K Pisi (G Dickson 64); Elliott, North, Burrell, Collins; Myler, Fotuali'i (L Dickson 72); A Waller (E Waller 65), Haywood (Hartley 57), Ma'afu (Mercey 57), Manoa (Lawes 64), Day, Clark (Dowson 64), Wood (c), Dickinson.

Referee: Matthew Carley

Attendance: 6,897

Tries: Saints: Christian Day

Penalties: Wasps: Elliot Daly, Andy Goode (2), Joe Carlisle (2).
Saints: Stephen Myler (4)

In truth, it was a game only a forwards coach could truly enjoy.

Plenty of scrummaging, plenty of mauling and not much else.

In fact, the medical team's main job was to make sure the wingers hadn't fallen asleep during the lengthy spells at the set piece.

Dorian West wouldn't have minded one bit.

But for Saints it was another vital victory in their quest to be top of the Premiership shop come the end of the season.

Saracens' crushing six-try success against Leicester means the men from Allianz Park are still the team to catch.

They have lost just once this season, and that was the demolition job Saints did on them at Franklin's Gardens at the end of October.

That may have been the last truly spectacular performance Saints put on in the Premiership, but, thankfully for Jim Mallinder's men, it wasn't the last time they won.

They have picked up three successive victories since then, none of them particularly pretty.

They have scrapped, shoved and eventually outgunned the opposition, which has comprised of Newcastle, Worcester and Wasps.

Saturday's win, secured by Stephen Myler's ice cool kick in blustery, wet conditions at Adams Park was, perhaps, the sweetest of them all.

The scrum penalty going Northampton's way in the final seconds may have been the rugby gods' way of evening out what happened at Gloucester back in September.

On that occasion, the Cherry and Whites were the ones celebrating a final-kick success.

This time, it was Northampton, who still only have that Kingsholm reverse in the games lost column in the league this season.

The ability to keep going to the last showed just how much character is in this Saints squad this season.

And when you add it to what happened a week earlier in Dublin, when Saints survived a late Leinster onslaught to land the final blow through Jamie Elliott's try, it is a hugely impressive result.

So often teams can suffer a European hangover.

They can hit their nadir just a week after reaching their apex.

But Mallinder's men are made of sterner stuff than that these days.

There was no repeat of what happened last year, when they won in Belfast only to suffer a tame defeat to Harlequins a week later.

No, this wasn't a performance on par with what we witnessed at the Aviva Stadium. But the outcome was the same.

By hook or by crook, Saints are finding ways to win games.

Whether it be through the power of their forwards or the precision of Myler's boot, they get the job done.

They even had to contend with some contentious officiating on this occasion, as the TMO and referee Matthew Carley did not have the best of days.

But even that couldn't stop Saints.

And although they are not No.1 at Christmas, the men from Northampton are not far off.

Cometh the hour, cometh the Iceman. That was how it panned out for Saints as they relied on their metronomic kicking king to get them over the line in a game full of plenty of huff and puff, but not much else.

From the highs of Dublin, this was a real comedown, but, crucially for Saints, they had once again pocketed the points they needed.

Saracens would stay top at Christmas, but Mallinder's men were hot on their heels thanks to the coolness of a fly half who had certainly stepped up to make the No.10 shirt his own, making memories of men such as Shane Geraghty and Ryan Lamb ever more distant.

'You need someone who's steady in those positions,' Mallinder said, after seeing Myler land the winning points with the final kick of a game Wasps had looked set to win thanks to Joe Carlisle's 78th-minute penalty.

'I don't really know what was going through Stephen's mind. I know what was going through mine as he kicked it. I'm delighted.

'He kicked well all game. It wasn't just that one. There were quite a lot of shots at goal where he did well.'

While Mallinder had a smile etched on his face, Wasps boss Young was reeling as his side suffered their ninth successive Saints defeat.

Young said he was 'gutted' and had some interesting things to say about Matthew Carley after the referee chose to award Saints a penalty at the game's final scrum, which allowed Myler to secure his status as match-winner.

'We hadn't beaten them for four seasons so with 30 seconds to go we thought we had done enough,' Young said.

'It took 80 minutes for a penalty to come from a scrum, which is remarkable. We had reset and reset all game and then in injury time we have one scrum which goes down and he [Carley] penalises us straight away. I can't see where that one came from at all really.

'We feel hugely disappointed because that was a game we had worked really hard to win.

'You don't get that opportunity against Northampton too often so I'm really proud of the players and I'm gutted for them because we had done enough to win that game.

'Northampton are an excellent team and well coached. We knew it was going to be a massive challenge for us but we stuck with it and with a minute to go they knock on and we had a clear advantage but he pulled us back for it. It was the first scrum a team had been done on the engagement.'

It mattered not to Saints as they backed up their big win in Ireland and looked forward to one more game in the calendar year, with Bath ready to try to finish their own 12 months on a high at the Gardens.

Mallinder moved to strengthen his squad before that match, and 2014, arrived, as Samoan utility back Fa'atoina Autagavaia – he was later to be nicknamed 'Fat Tony' as Saints fans adapted his name to a more manageable pronunciation – was drafted in as cover for knee injury victim Foden.

Wilson was also out, meaning Ken Pisi had been covering at full back, so the arrival of Autagavaia, a try-scorer for Samoa against Wales in November 2012, provided a useful extra option for Mallinder as he sought to maintain his team's momentum.

More Samoan smiles were to come in the form of George Pisi, who was back from his ban for the game against Bath, while another five contract renewals were confirmed, with Foden, Elliott, Burrell, Ken Pisi and Lee Dickson putting pen to paper on Christmas Eve.

The news provided yet more welcome festive gifts for Saints supporters and there was real cheer around the Gardens as Bath made their way to the ground for the final fixture of a year that had seen Northampton come a long way. All that was needed now was a happy ending.

Game 17: Saturday, 28 December 2013: Northampton Saints 43 Bath 25 (Aviva Premiership – round 11)

Saints: K Pisi (Collins 47); Elliott, G Pisi (G Dickson 75), Burrell, North; Myler, Fotuali'i (L Dickson 62); A Waller (E Waller 62), Hartley (c) (Haywood 69), Ma'afu (Mercey 52), Lawes, Day (Dickinson 69), Clark (Dowson 64), Wood, Manoa.

Bath: Watson; Agulla (Abendanon 62), Joseph, Eastmond, Banahan; Ford, Roberts (Stringer 46); James (Catt 58), Webber (Guinazu 62), Perenise (Orlandi 52), Hooper (c) (Day 52), Attwood, Garvey, Louw, Fearns (Houston 46).

Referee: Luke Pearce (replaced by Martin Fox inside two minutes)

Attendance: 13,475

Tries: Saints: Christian Day (2), George Pisi, Jamie Elliott, Samu Manoa, George North. **Bath:** Kyle Eastmond, Rob Webber, Leroy Houston

Conversions: Saints: Stephen Myler (5). **Bath:** George Ford (2)

Penalties: Saints: Stephen Myler. **Bath:** George Ford (2)

They might have started like stuffed turkeys, but Saints eventually served up a showing to be proud of in Saturday's 43-25 win against Bath.

It was yet another devastating example of just how slick Jim Mallinder's men can be and, at their best, they are proving hugely difficult to stop.

Another six tries, against a side who had won their previous 11 games in all competitions, kept the heat on Saracens at the top of the Premiership standings.

As Bath boss Mike Ford pointed out, the top two are in a league of their own currently, with others playing catch-up.

But just as impressive as the results they are getting is the manner in which Saints are recording them.

In the past few weeks they have been presented with different shaped obstacles, successfully navigating a way past each of them. No, they didn't play to their best for the full 80 minutes – as they did at Leinster – in the victories against Wasps and Bath, but they have overcome adversity to prevail.

In a real forwards' battle at Adams Park, they found a way of winning, eventually, through Stephen Myler's boot.

And having gone 13-0 down inside 15 minutes at Franklin's Gardens on Saturday, they could have crumbled.

It could have been a Leinster-like struggle. Another crushing defeat that would leave Northampton needing to bounce back a week later.

But Saints showed they have learned from that home humbling. And learning quickly from your mistakes is the sign of a top team.

They showed, this time, they wouldn't be overawed. That an early deficit was not going to blow them away.

No, this team is growing week by week, with each individual player progressing hugely.

Jamie Elliott is one of those on the steepest of upward curves, with his attacking and defensive instincts now razor sharp.

It's easy to forget he's just 21, which is the same age as fellow winger George North.

The Wales star was the catalyst for this victory, dragging his team back into the game by the scruff of the neck.

A tackle in the air fired him up. Bath had stirred up a hornets' nest.

North went on to excel in every department and deservedly grabbed a try to put the icing on his and Saints' cake.

Luther Burrell was a big presence, Stephen Myler put the boot into Bath from the tee, Kahn Fotuali'i continued to enhance his burgeoning reputation.

The superlatives are running out.

If there was one area of weakness, though, it was the scrum, where Bath got the better of Saints to earn a string of penalties.

Christian Day stressed that part of his team's play must improve for the next game, against Harlequins on Friday night.

The wily campaigner is not getting too carried away.

And rightly so, as the turn of the year does not yield trophies, just expectations about what could lie ahead.

It is clear there is still a long way to go this season, but Saints issued another big statement of intent on Saturday.

Their Premiership home record this season is nothing short of incredible, with five tries scored against Exeter and Sale and six against both Saracens and Bath.

Throw in the Newcastle game, in which they scored twice, and Saints have racked up 24 scores in just five league matches on their own turf during this campaign.

The Leinster blip aside, they have shown all the hallmarks of a team who should not only expect to challenge come May, but who should expect to claim silverware. Yes, there's a long way to go, but, as they say, time flies when you're having fun.

And Saints players and supporters are certainly having plenty of that at the moment.

This was to be yet another pointer of a happy new year as Saints bounced back from 13-0 down to put a Bath team buzzing with belief to the sword with a mesmerising display.

Christian Day may have scored the most tries, with the lock bagging a brace, but North was the one attracting the majority of the praise in the post-match press conference.

'George was outstanding,' said Mallinder. 'He got us going after that first ten, 15 minutes.

'He got us on the front foot with his carrying, he got us on the front foot with his high balls and to see his defensive work in the 80th minute to cut them out there was great.

'It's taken him a bit of time, but he's showing why he's a world class player.'

Prior to this match, North had been issuing some praise of his own, thanking the Saints supporters for making him feel so welcome in Northampton and hailing the club for the flexibility they had given him when it came to international duty.

So flexible had Saints been that they were forced to pay a one-off £60,000 fine, which had been issued by Premiership Rugby for the club allowing North to play for Wales against Australia on 30 November, contrary to a Premiership clubs' agreement that only England players could be released for matches outside of the international window.

That backing to be allowed to play for his national team whenever he wanted was part of the reason North had opted to join Saints – and they were reaping the rewards of his decision.

He had shown he was worth every penny of that hefty fine with the big display against Bath and it helped Saints head into 2014 on the back of a three-match winning streak.

Bath boss Mike Ford had admitted that Mallinder's men would take some stopping, saying the team from Northampton and the one known as Saracens appeared to be in a league of their own.

Those two teams looked like they were on an inevitable collision course in a campaign that had seen both clubs showcase their credentials on a weekly basis.

Next up for Saints was a first game of the new year, against Harlequins, who were gunning for revenge having been beaten on their own turf by Northampton during the formative stages of the season.

In the build-up to the game, Burrell had warned that Quins were a much improved side from the one he and his team-mates had seen off in September and the big centre was looking to further his England aims by helping to slay them once again.

He knew it would be another big personal statement and yet another warning to the league should Saints overcome the 2012 champions.

Quins, Leicester and Saracens had joined Saints as part of an established top four in recent seasons, but the team from Northampton had found a way to avoid defeat against their main rivals.

None of them had managed to beat Mallinder's men thus far during the campaign and that record needed to continue if it was to be a winning start to 2014 for one of 2013's most impressive teams.

Game 18: Friday, 3 January 2014: Northampton Saints 23 Harlequins 9 (Aviva Premiership – round 12)

Saints: Collins (Autagavaia 75); Elliott, G Pisi, Burrell, North; Myler (G Dickson 75), L Dickson (Fotuali'i 61); A Waller (E Waller 67), Hartley (c) (Haywood 73), Ma'afu (Mercey 67), Lawes, Day, Clark, Dowson (Wood 60), Manoa (Dickinson 75).

Harlequins: Brown; Walker, Hopper, Molenaar, Smith (Lindsay-Hague 75); Evans (Botica 40), K Dickson; Marler (Lambert 73), Ward, Collier (Doran-Jones 67), Matthews (Kennedy 55), Robson, Guest (Trayfoot 61), Robshaw (c), Easter.

Referee: Greg Garner

Attendance: 13,475

Tries: Saints: George North, Dylan Hartley

Conversions: Saints: Stephen Myler (2)

Penalties: Saints: Stephen Myler (3). **Harlequins:** Nick Evans (2), Ben Botica

To borrow some football terminology, Harlequins seemed to come for the draw at Franklin's Gardens on Friday night.

So it is to Saints' credit that they overcame a team whose disruption and delay made for a first half played at a snail's pace.

Quins, aware that their hosts had won all five of their Premiership home games to that point, and in style, took their time to get to the line-out and set up for scrums.

They aimed to take any possible flow out of Northampton and, for the first 40 minutes, it worked.

The teams headed in at half-time level at 6-6 in a fixture that was shaping up to be similar to the one between the sides at the Gardens last year, when Quins claimed an 18-9 win.

Then, Nick Evans landed six penalties in a stagnant affair, and Saints were desperate to avoid a repeat on this occasion. That they did owed much to their new-found belief, their power game and the increased threat in the back line this season. George North plays a big part in that, and the Wales wing's try, which saw him brush aside England hopeful Charlie Walker on the way to the line, was a moment for Saints fans to savour.

As he did in the reverse fixture at The Stoop, North brought the game to life, showing just why he is worth the money Saints shelled out to bring him to the Gardens.

Captain Dylan Hartley was the leader of a pack that played the power game superbly, with Calum Clark among the others upping the intensity to a level Quins couldn't cope with.

In the end, the away team didn't even have a losing bonus point to show for their efforts.

But they are not the first side to suffer that fate.

Saints have played six home games in the Premiership this season, and no opposition outfit has left with anything other than a bruised ego.

The teams who have fared best at the Gardens have taken a different approach to Quins, who, it has to be said, saw their game plan aided by some indecisive officiating.

Leinster claimed a 40-7 win in the Heineken Cup thanks to a fast-paced start, keeping Saints on the back foot from the off.

Bath, too, looked sharp as they surged into a 13-0 lead and Sale were another side who attempted to play Saints at their own game early on.

On the flip side, Newcastle and Quins came to frustrate, trying to stay in the game for as long as possible before attempting to spring a surprise.

It didn't work.

Saints have become an all-weather side, who find ways to win in whatever conditions they are presented with.

It is the sign of a team with strengths across the park, a team with immense capability in every department.

Saints are very similar to Saracens in that respect and that is why those two teams are currently well clear of the rest in the Premiership standings.

Hartley stood in the small room situated next to the Gardens dressing room ready to conduct his interview. The skipper was covered, head to toe, in mud, having shown his battling qualities in a bruising forward display against Harlequins.

Hartley was a picture of fight and determination, and the dirt that adorned his shirt was a symbol of the kind of game Saints had been involved in, needing every ounce of spirit to overcome a stubborn Harlequins side.

The forwards ground Quins down while the backs tried to find a way through, but, with the conditions not conducive to a game ruled by the smaller men on the field, it was all about who had the most power.

Thankfully for Saints, it was they who showed the greater muscle, with Hartley leading the forward effort and North again lighting up a match with a moment to remember.

The Wales wing had broken the Quins resistance with a typically rambunctious run that saw Charlie Walker thrust into the car headlights.

It was like watching a worm dropped into the road before being run over by a monster truck, and it got Saints up and running in a second half that saw them push on and get the points they needed to prevail once again.

'We needed it,' said Mallinder of North's big moment. 'George was one-on-one and it was a fantastic effort.

'It was against young [Charlie] Walker, who is a talented player, but George, one-on-one, you've got to make sure you make a good tackle. To see him go in the corner was fantastic.'

Saints had now savoured two wins against a club who had inflicted plenty of pain on them in previous years and it was the perfect way to start a 12-month period that many were predicting would be 'the year of the Saint'.

'It's pleasing [to have done the double over Harlequins] because there was all that chat last year about us not beating [top four] teams and it hurt,' Mallinder added.

'We're delighted we've done the double over Quins and we've beaten Bath and beaten Saracens here. That's good for us and this is a good start to the new year for us.'

That good start was about to be tested, with two European fixtures lying in wait during the weeks that followed. Ospreys and Castres were on the agenda, with Saints, who were four points adrift of Leinster, needing to win both matches to keep any hopes of progressing past the group stages alive.

There would be a five-day turnaround from the trip to Wales to the home game against the French team, meaning the squad would be put to the test in the bid to reach the quarter-finals for the first time since the 2010/11 season.

Injury fears over Myler, who had kicked 13 points against Quins, and Lawes were eventually allayed as things started to hot up ahead of a must-win match at the Liberty Stadium.

Skipper Hartley was keeping his team-mates' heads focused solely on the weekend's game, urging them not to worry about making the quarter-finals, while forwards coach West was busy disputing suggestions that his team would face an Ospreys outfit with nothing to play for.

Ospreys had only won one of their four matches in the Heineken Cup, but West said: 'I've read a few interviews that some of their staff and players have done and they're thinking they can win a couple of games and have a result go their way in the others games and still qualify for the Amlin [Challenge Cup].

'They'll be full on to beat us, that's certainly how we're preparing and it will be a really tough challenge.'

Saints would have expected nothing less in European rugby's premier club competition, and Ospreys had certainly been competitive in their 26-17 defeat at the Gardens a few months earlier.

Just as on that October occasion, there was huge pressure on Mallinder's men to perform as they sought to make sure the win in Dublin wasn't worthless.

That December night was mentioned more than a few times in the Gardens corridors before the trip to Wales and there was a strong determination to replicate the Irish invasion with a similar showing across the Severn.

Game 19: Sunday, 12 January 2014: Ospreys 17 Northampton Saints 29 (Heineken Cup pool stages – game five)

Ospreys: Fussell; Hassler, Isaacs (John 65), Spratt, Natoga; Biggar, Webb; Bevington, Hibbard (Baldwin 55), Jarvis (A Jones 46), A W Jones (c), Evans (King 64), Lewis (Allen 52), Tipuric, Bearman.

Saints: Collins (Autagavaia 40); Elliott, G Pisi, Burrell, North; Myler (G Dickson 72), Fotuali'i (L Dickson 56); A Waller (E Waller 64), Hartley (c) (Haywood 72), Ma'afu (Mercey 52), Lawes, Day, Clark (Dowson 60), Wood (Dickinson 73), Manoa.

Referee: Pascal Gauzere (France)

Attendance: 8,347

Tries: Ospreys: Rhys Webb, Alun Wyn Jones. **Saints:** George North, George Pisi, Glenn Dickson

Conversions: Ospreys: Dan Biggar (2). **Saints:** Glenn Dickson

Penalties: Ospreys: Dan Biggar. **Saints:** Stephen Myler (4)

A slim chance of progression and a stadium with little atmosphere can be a dangerous proposition.

Just ask the Saints of January 2012, who headed to Glasgow's Scotstoun knowing they needed to at least win to stand any chance of progressing to the Heineken Cup last eight. On that occasion, Jim Mallinder's men played a fast and loose game, gunning for the four-try bonus point from the off.

Eventually, though, they paid the price for their unlimited adventure, losing with the last play of the game as Glasgow Warriors' Peter Horne danced in for a fatal try.

Saints lost the game, their hopes of participation in any European competition in tatters.

Their ambition was to be applauded, but the way they applied themselves was perhaps slightly unstructured and they struggled to turn possession into points.

Not on Sunday in Swansea, though.

Saints were methodical, shooting down the Ospreys with a display that never really allowed the opposition the sort of sniff Glasgow were given. Metronome Stephen Myler kept the scoreboard ticking over before George North, George Pisi and Glenn Dickson got over the line after the break.

Ospreys responded, as you would expect most home teams in the Heineken Cup to, but they never looked likely to claim a win.

For the second time in Pool 1, they had given Northampton a game, but found themselves at arm's length throughout it.

This Saints team allies belief with strength on the road, and Sunday's display showed how far they had come since the Scotstoun suffering.

The fact they are unlikely to make it through to the Heineken Cup last eight is a let-off for the teams who do.

Because Saints, who would be on the road in the quarter-finals should Ospreys spring the biggest of surprises in Dublin and Castres capitulate in Northampton on Friday, can beat anyone on their travels on their day.

Just ask Saracens, after last May's Premiership play-off semi-final.

Ask Leinster, after that Aviva Stadium stunner.

And ask this Ospreys team, who, despite only having claimed five points in the pool, are no mugs. They are third in the RaboDirect PRO12 and have a number of Lions in their squad.

It will be a great shame that this Saints team will not be able to show what they can do in the latter stages of the competition.

But, if as expected they don't make it, they cannot blame anyone other than themselves, after two defeats from the first three games.

The Castres loss always looked likely to be costly, while the defeat to Leinster at the Gardens seemed to be a knock-out blow.

That is wasn't at the time is credit to this Saints team, who have rebuilt to great effect since that night at the Gardens, winning their next five games.

Sunday's success was earned through desire and a determination not to go quietly in Europe this season.

Skipper Dylan Hartley drove his players on. There was a dollop of determination put into every ruck.

The visiting forwards bossed proceedings, taking Ospreys to task in the scrum, giving the ever-impressive back line the chance to pounce. And pounce they did, with North lighting up the encounter, giving those fans who did take the plunge and make it to the Liberty Stadium a moment to savour.

The travelling Saints fans had earned it, and the Wales star continues on his steep upward curve.

Three tries in three games show his worth, but that record doesn't fully illustrate the contribution of a player who has been a catalyst for his new team's development.

This breed of Saints are learning quickly and the past year has seen a real progression.

They might not get to cap that as Heineken Cup champions, but don't bet against them lifting a different type of European trophy this season.

Aviva Stadium-style fireworks were hardly expected in Swansea, but North did at least provide another eye-catching rocket as he once again shot Saints to victory in a European encounter.

The Welshman, back in the country he represents internationally, lit up a turgid clash with a moment of magic that ensured Saints kept their Heineken Cup flame flickering.

They would need a favour on the following weekend, when they would host Castres and Leinster would entertain Ospreys and, though it seemed unlikely, at least they had not wilted under the pressure and at least they maintained their ever-increasing momentum.

Mallinder once again found himself hailing North, talking about a 'quality try' and discussing just how well North was fitting in during his first season at Franklin's Gardens.

It was the powerhouse wing's third try in as many matches, and they were hardly one-metre pushovers. He was opening teams up with trademark big bursts, and clubs were struggling to stop him.

North, a former Scarlets player, savoured the part he was able to play in Saints' south Wales success, making up for a lack of luck at the Liberty Stadium in the colours of his old club.

'I've been here many times but not come away with the win so it was nice to put one on the Ospreys as an ex-Scarlet,' he said after the game.

North was coming into form at the right time, helping Saints to kick on during the middle of the campaign, and the club would need him to be at his special best if they were to get the bonus-point win they desperately wanted against Castres on the following Friday.

Saints had the scent of revenge in their nostrils ahead of that game, with Burrell expressing a strong desire to secure the full five points to make sure his side had done everything they could to overhaul Leinster at the top of Pool 1.

However, whatever was to happen in the final round of pool matches, the players were keen to point out that they would deal with it head on.

Should it be the Challenge Cup, so be it, said Dickinson as he took on pre-match media duties. Saints simply wanted European glory, and if it wouldn't come in the Heineken Cup, they were confident it would happen in the lesser of the two tournaments on the continent.

'It would be taken on as a brand new challenge,' Dickinson said, in upbeat fashion. 'It will be disappointing if we are out of the Heineken Cup, but we'll take that just as seriously and that will be the next target to win.'

Pre-season expectations had been that the club could compete at the top table in Europe, though, and the supporters were craving a big performance at Franklin's Gardens to finish an onerous pool stage.

Myler stressed that keeping the five-match winning run going was the most important thing, no matter how Saints did it against a Castres side who would need a big win to move above their English opponents into second.

Never knowing what kind of challenge a French team with little to play for will pose in the latter stages of the Heineken Cup, everyone at Franklin's Gardens prepared themselves for a big challenge and demanded that the job got done in the best fashion possible.

Autagavaia was brought in for his first start in the green, black and gold, as he replaced Collins at full back, and Wood handed his team a big boost by shaking off a knock to take his place in the starting 15.

Serving up revenge on a cold Northampton night was the aim, and Saints knew they had to achieve it if they wanted to continue their European journey in a campaign that was promising to add plenty of silverware to the Gardens trophy cabinet.

Game 20: Friday, 17 January 2014: Northampton Saints 13 Castres Olympique 3 (Heineken Cup pool stages – game six)

Saints: Autagavaia (G Dickson 68); K Pisi, G Pisi, Burrell (Waldouck 62), North; Myler, L Dickson (Fotuali'i 55); A Waller (E Waller 61), Hartley (c) (Haywood 61), Ma'afu (Denman 51), Lawes, Day, Clark (Dowson 54), Wood, Manoa (Dickinson 61).

Castres: Dulin; Garvey (Lakafia 68), Cabannes (c), Lamerat (Bonnefond 62), Grosso; Kirkpatrick, Tomas (Kockott 51); Forestier, Rallier (Taumopeau 51), Peikrishvili (Lazar 27), Samson, Gray, Babillot (Desroche 63), Bornman, Faasalele (Caballero 40).

Referee: Alain Rolland

Attendance: 12,302

Tries: Saints: George Pisi

Conversions: Saints: Glenn Dickson

Penalties: Saints: Stephen Myler (2). **Castres:** Rory Kockott

---

If there is to be no Heineken Cup next season, one small crumb of comfort will be that Saints won't have to meet Castres again.

Because of the eight meetings between the sides in the past four seasons, very few have been memorable affairs.

The French team have represented a sizeable stumbling block for Saints, who have failed to make it out of the pool stages in the past three campaigns. When they did progress to the last eight, in the 2010/11 season, they won in France as part of a 100 per cent pool stage record on the road to the final at the Millennium Stadium in Cardiff.

They won't be back there this year, though, and one of the reasons for that is the French resistance.

Jim Mallinder gave an honest assessment of his team's travails after Friday night's turgid win against Castres at Franklin's Gardens.

He said the lack of an Italian side in the pool proved pivotal. And he's right as the best runner-up spots will go to teams in the pools containing Zebre and Treviso.

But the presence of Castres has proved even more important, because had they not seen off Saints in round one and stopped them getting a try bonus point at the Gardens it would be an entirely different story.

As it is, the next trip on the European agenda is set to be one with an Amlin Challenge Cup flavour.

That will taste sour for now, but come April it will be another chance to win silverware.

It wasn't what Saints, who have won 16 of their 20 games in all competitions this season, were hoping for as they, rightly, target the biggest pots these days.

They should have beaten Castres away and they should not have lost so heavily to Leinster at the Gardens.

But then you may not have thought they would win in Dublin and proceed to hold Ospreys at arm's length in Swansea.

It has been a six-game campaign of peaks and troughs, with plenty of points in the lessons learned column.

Unfortunately, once more, Castres have helped ensure there aren't quite enough points in the column that matters most.

'Come on, Connacht!' Those were the first words that a jovial Mallinder uttered in his press conference after what was an energy-sapping encounter for all involved at the Gardens.

The director of rugby was clinging to his side's final hope, which was that Saracens lost at home to Connacht and Cardiff Blues failed to win their home clash with Exeter Chiefs, as well as other favourable scorelines elsewhere.

Leinster had won Pool 1 because, as expected, they dismissed Ospreys in Dublin to ensure they would secure their place in the last eight, leaving everyone in Northampton waiting for the outcome of matches elsewhere. In the end, it wasn't to be, as Saracens and Leicester Tigers stole the final two best runners-up spots to join Leinster, Ulster, Clermont Auvergne, Toulon, Munster and Toulouse in the battle for European supremacy.

Saints were given the scenario they had already been steeling themselves for: a Challenge Cup clash, which was to have all the glamour of a greasy spoon as they were handed a Thursday night trip to Sale Sharks in the last eight.

However, at least they had done their job against Castres. It still inspired some regret as there was a palpable feeling of disappointment that they had not been able to do the same in France, losing a game they should never have lost.

In the end, that Stade Pierre Antoine agony in October would be left to eat away at the team as they dropped into the Challenge Cup, but the revenge mission had been completed and the winning run had been extended to six matches, meaning the return to Premiership matters would be a smooth one.

The victory against Castres failed to capture the imagination as it was to turn out to be something of a damp squib that left the Gardens faithful desperate for it to end, with only George Pisi's try providing any real reason to cheer.

It was another win though and it was one that left Hartley dreaming of Cardiff glory in a different form, saying 'there's another tournament to be played in now, another trophy to win and we'll give it a good crack'. That message would be replicated a few times in the days to come as Saints turned their attentions to another competition, the LV= Cup.

Unlike in the Heineken-sponsored tournament, they were not having to use January to play catch-up as they were sitting pretty at the top of Pool 4.

A trip to Newport Gwent Dragons was next on the Anglo-Welsh agenda and the players on the fringe of the side licked their lips in anticipation of a trip to Rodney Parade, which could provide a platform for a place in the semi-finals.

For the team's big names, big games beckoned on the international scene, with a host of players looking forward to representing England.

Flanker Calum Clark would be given the Saxons captaincy as he led a squad that also contained Alex Waller, Dickinson and Mercey, while Burrell, Hartley, Lawes, Wood, Lee Dickson and Myler were heading to Pennyhill Park to join up with the senior squad ahead of the start of the Six Nations Championship.

Saints were without 15 players for the journey to Wales, with Dowson the man given the responsibility of steering the side to another victory against a Newport team they were still expected to beat.

Heading to Rodney Parade on the back of Heineken Cup action at the Gardens was a bit like eating a Burger King just after tickling your taste buds at a fancy restaurant, but there was still that real appetite to gobble up whatever trophies were on offer.

There would be no telling the shadow squad players that this competition did not matter as it was their chance to prove themselves, and that was exactly what they had done in the November wins against Gloucester and London Irish, scoring tries for fun.

Saints had won at Rodney Parade during a state of flux in the previous season, but this time they were a far more settled bunch, with every squad member buying into what was turning into a success story. Mallinder was insisting that his team were capable of competing on all three fronts, saying: 'It's tough, but it's where we want to be. We have got a big squad and we have got some very big players.

'We want to be playing rugby every week, we don't want weeks off. We'd rather channel ourselves, see if we can rotate our squad, keep everybody fresh and it is a challenge to us as management to make sure that, if we do get into semi-finals and finals, our players are fresh enough and ready to go and win those big games.'

Mallinder's confidence was echoed by Glenn Dickson, who was setting his sights on securing a home semi-final during the next two weeks, with a home game against Saracens to come after the bid to slay the Dragons.

'The next two weeks are extremely important,' Dickson said.

That sentence simply summed up the importance the Kiwi and his team-mates were placing on continuing their club's good run and cementing places in the first-team picture for the three trophy tilts.

Game 21: Saturday, 25 January 2014: Newport Gwent Dragons 16 Northampton Saints 34 (LV= Cup pool stages – game three)

Newport Gwent Dragons: Evans; Pewtner (Wardle 11), Leach, Smith, Harries; Tovey (Burton 47), L Jones (Rees 47); Price (Evans 51), Dee (Thomas 47), Buck (Mills 57), Hill, A Jones (Screech 35), L Evans (c), Benjamin (Groves 57), Talei.

Saints: Wilson; K Pisi, Stephenson, Waldouck, Autagavaia; G Dickson (Olver 70), Fotuali'i (A Day 70); E Waller (Hobbs-Awoyemi 65), Haywood (McMillan 65), Denman (Parkins 65), Verbakel, C Day, Harrison (Nutley 65), Dowson (c) (Williams 66), van Velze.

Referee: Andrew Small

Attendance: 6,011

Tries: Newport Gwent Dragons: Luc Jones. **Saints:** Penalty try, Fa'atoina Autagavaia, Mike Haywood, Gareth Denman, GJ van Velze

Conversions: Newport Gwent Dragons: Jason Tovey. **Saints:** Glenn Dickson (3)

Penalties: Newport Gwent Dragons: Jason Tovey (3). **Saints:** Glenn Dickson

---

Towards the end of Saturday's game at Rodney Parade conditions were more akin to a swimming gala than a rugby match.

But, once again, Saints showcased their effective all-weather game as they scrapped to a 34-16 win against a struggling Newport side.

The hosts, who shipped 19 unanswered points in the second half, were less fire-breathing Dragons, more unicorns as they failed to match Northampton's power game.

Lyn Jones's men were drowned by a Saints pack who were totally dominant, upping the intensity levels after the break to secure a third win from as many games in this season's LV= Cup.

The statistics are startling, with Saints having scored a whopping 106 points in three Anglo-Welsh outings, despite missing the majority of their first 15.

What is evident is that the winning ethos and strong style of play runs right throughout the club.

There are almost three sets of players capable of stepping up and producing big performances when it matters.

And there are senior players, such as the ever-impressive Christian Day and Phil Dowson, who help the youngsters understand what it means to be a Saint.

It is a luxurious position for director of rugby Jim Mallinder to be in as he blends youth with experience and continues to get results.

Mallinder has steered his side to 17 wins and a draw from their 21 games in all competitions this season, with only three teams – Castres, Gloucester and Leinster – earning victories. It is a sensational record that illustrates the strength in depth that Saints now possess, and their ability to survive in the most extreme of circumstances.

That adaptability was on show to the maximum at Rodney Parade on a day when the wind, rain and hail was so severe that referee Andrew Small had to pull the players off the pitch.

Saints, after a quick warm-up exercise at the interval, made their way through the monsoon to drive home their quality in the second 40 minutes.

Their maul was irresistible, their scrum unstoppable and their half-backs intelligent on a day when the Dragons crumbled under the strain.

Home head coach Jones admitted his side had been taught a harsh lesson, but they weren't the first to see the Saints machine roll into town and proceed to flatten the opposition.

The green, black and gold now have a home semi-final in their sights, with a victory against Saracens at Franklin's Gardens next weekend crucial to making that hope a reality.

And you would certainly have to be of a brave disposition to bet against Saints achieving it.

Just ask Jones and his Dragons.

While the previous few weeks had seen North and Co. running riot, Saints were forced to show the other side of their game at Rodney Parade.

In horrendous conditions, their pack turned up the heat to stave off the challenge of the Dragons, ploughing through the mud to claim another comfortable LV= Cup victory.

The picture of tighthead prop Denman sliding through the mud to score summed things up perfectly as Saints adjusted to the conditions and pulled well clear during the second period.

Mallinder's mood after the game was one of a schoolteacher who had seen his team pass an exam that they could never have revised for, and he admitted his shock at the conditions in which the match had been played, with severe hail and lightning forcing the players off the pitch at one point.

'I've played and been involved in some snowstorms, some hailstorms but never as severe as that,' the former Sale full back had said after the game.

'To see players in open play turning round and not looking at the ball was incredible. The referee did the right thing to get off for a few minutes and then continue.

'It was difficult. We'd said before the game that it wasn't a bad day. We'd talked about it being bad conditions but when we first came out it was just a little bit of wind, a bit wet underfoot but generally fine.

'It wasn't until the hail and the rain came down and the lads were actually in the changing rooms shivering. It all makes me even more proud of the players and the way they played.'

Amid the weather chaos, the experience of men such as Christian Day and Dowson came to the fore as they steered the younger players into the right positions, acting as stewards among the pack.

Day, who described conditions as 'like something you see on TV when they're doing a documentary about the Arctic', felt it was a valuable experience for the team's fledgling players and there could be no doubt that they had coped admirably with all of the mud that had been slung in their direction.

It was yet another win to keep the Saints steamroller going and they were so close to securing a home semi-final in the LV= Cup. They knew a win against Saracens on the following weekend would get the job done and complete a flawless pool stage.

Myler was back in the squad for that encounter, having missed out on a place in the England party for the Six Nations Championship opener against France, but he wouldn't start, with Will Hooley brought in to make his debut at fly half.

Another Northampton player making a first start that weekend was Luther Burrell as he was given the nod for England in Paris, while Hartley, Lawes, Wood and Dickson would also be kept on by head coach Lancaster in the build-up to the Stade de France showdown.

For Saints, there was just one more LV= Cup hurdle to negotiate before the return to league action, and there was a real feeling that Saracens would go the same way as London Irish, Gloucester and Newport Gwent Dragons had done.

Saints scrum half Alex Day stoked the fires by pointing out that two of Sarries' four defeats since the previous April had come at the hands of Northampton, and he was confident his side could continue their good record against their rivals.

It would be the latest instalment of the thrilling battle for supremacy that the two clubs were engaging in and if Saints could again get the win, there was every chance they would face Saracens in the semi-finals little more than a month later.

Game 22: Saturday, 1 February 2014: Northampton Saints 20 Saracens 16 (LV= Cup pool stages – game four)

Saints: Wilson; Elliott, G Pisi (Autagavaia 62), Waldouck, K Pisi; Hooley (Myler 64), Fotuali'i, E Waller (Warren 65), Haywood (McMillan 67), Denman (Parkins 56), Verbakel (Day 54), Manoa, Harrison (Williams 54), Nutley, van Velze.

Saracens: Ransom; Tagicakibau, Streather (Stanley 1), Bosch, Wilson; Mordt, Spencer; Gill (Barrington 30), Saunders (Spurling 54), Du Plessis, Smith (Botha 54), Sheriff, de Jaeger (Burger 54), Hankin, Melck (Jubb 72).

Referee: JP Doyle

Attendance: 13,256

Tries: Saints: James Wilson, Samu Manoa (2). **Saracens:** Ben Spencer

Conversions: Saints: Will Hooley. **Saracens:** Ben Spencer

Penalties: Saints: Will Hooley. **Saracens:** Ben Spencer (3)

Saints have now won their past three games against Saracens – and Samu Manoa has stamped his authority on each one of them.

Saracens players are to Manoa what a red rag is to a bull, with the American displaying extreme intensity levels every time he faces the men from north London.

Last May, he was a picture of strength as he bulldozed Northampton into the Premiership Final at the expense of Saracens at Allianz Park.

Then, in October, he was once again named man of the match as Sarries were slayed 41-20 at Franklin's Gardens.

And he was at it again on Saturday, dragging a Saints team lacking some inspiration towards a home semi-final.

Manoa's performance was as huge as his frame, scoring twice and helping to set up the first score for James Wilson.

Saracens simply could not cope with the forward, who turned his hand to playing at lock rather than at No.8, where he has been plying his trade of late.

Manoa gave impetus to a Saints team who were crying out for it.

Saracens had taken a 16-15 lead going into the game's final stages and looked set to host Saints in the semi-finals on the second weekend of March.

Enter Manoa, who bulldozed his way over the line for the second time during the second half, and Saints turned the tables, switching the final-four tie to the Gardens.

It gives them a great chance of making the Sandy Park showpiece and claiming the first silverware of the season.

That would provide the perfect platform for a push in the Aviva Premiership and Amlin Challenge Cup.

And if Saints are to have a shot at each of those trophies, they will need their Californian crusher to continue his hugely impressive form.

Manoa had become one of few Saints players with his own chant – to the tune of The White Stripes' 'Seven Nation Army' – and it was easy to see why, as he once again swatted away Saracens with a huge display.

His class came to the fore to help ensure Saints would enjoy a home semi-final and, to the glee of the big American, he would be able to get stuck into Saracens again in the not too distant future as it was the Barnet-based club who would provide the opposition in the final four.

On this occasion, Saints had to battle so hard to get the result they wanted, but, by this point, they were simply forgetting how to lose games.

Tricky obstacles would be thrown in their path, but they would negotiate them, like an expert Mario Kart player dodging his way around the track.

Saints may still have been sitting three points behind table-topping Saracens in the Premiership standings when this game took place, but they ensured they would finish ahead of their rivals in the LV= Cup pool thanks to this Manoa-inspired success.

Hooley showed his character on debut, overcoming a couple of early missed kicks to help propel his team to victory, with Myler coming on for the final 15 minutes to shore things up.

Across the Channel, Burrell was unable to enjoy a similar winning debut, but he did write his name in the headlines with a try against the French, displaying the quality that everyone in Northampton knew he had.

The big centre was setting himself up for a big Six Nations Championship, meaning his club would have to do without him for some weeks yet, but Manoa was beating the drum, urging his team-mates to 'hold it down until the big boys come back'.

He had certainly led by example against Saracens and the gargantuan forward was now rubbing his hands at the prospect of taking down Exeter Chiefs at Sandy Park on the following weekend.

Ahead of that game, it was announced that van Velze would be leaving the club during the summer, with Worcester Warriors his destination, but movement off the field was not allowed to affect focus on it.

Saints knew that the Chiefs posed a real threat to their incredible unbeaten run, which had now reached eight matches, and they steeled themselves for the challenge of one of the Premiership's most improved outfits.

Haywood warned that the trip to the West Country would be a 'step up' for Saints, but forward coach West, who had spent the week sparring with Sky Sports pundit Pat Sanderson, who had accused Northampton of illegal scrummaging, backed his squad to stand up to the test once again.

'We've got a strong squad that can compete,' said West, who had seen Saints endure dips in form during previous Six Nations Championship spells. 'We feel more confident than we have done in the past in this period, but that's only in the back of your mind.

'You've got to go there, you've got to produce the goods and put in a real good performance to get past a top Exeter team.'

West's confidence was supported by the stunning record of 18 wins in the 22 previous games during the campaign and though seven England players as well as Wales star North would be missing, there was a real belief about the players as they started their long journey to Sandy Park.

Winger Ken Pisi was drawing on previous experiences to give himself a shot in the arm as he looked back on the win at Exeter during the previous season and the huge victory against them on the opening day of the current one.

'We've been on an awesome run recently and hopefully that can continue,' Pisi said. 'The boys have been playing their parts and we're enjoying it.'

But would Saints still be enjoying their recent unbeatable status after the game? One thing was for sure, it would take another special, characterful performance to protect it at what was a real Premiership stronghold.

Game 23: Saturday, 8 February 2014: Exeter Chiefs 16 Northampton Saints 17 (Aviva Premiership – round 13)

Exeter Chiefs: Arscott; Jess, Whitten, Dollman, James; Steenson, Lewis (Thomas 65); Moon, Yeandle (Cowan-Dickie 61), Brown (Tui 54), Mumm (c) (Armand 66), Welch, Ewers, Scaysbrook (Johnson 53), Horstmann.

Saints: Wilson; K Pisi, G Pisi, Waldouck (Hooley 67), Elliott; Myler, Fotuali'i; A Waller (E Waller 68), Haywood, Ma'afu (Denman 52), Manoa, C Day (van Velze 32), Clark, Dowson (c), Dickinson.

Referee: Greg Garner

Attendance: 8,336

Tries: Exeter Chiefs: Dave Lewis. **Saints:** James Wilson, Samu Manoa, George Pisi

Conversions: Exeter Chiefs: Gareth Steenson. **Saints:** Stephen Myler

Penalties: Exeter Chiefs: Gareth Steenson (3)

Saints have enjoyed some exceptional wins this season – and the one they achieved at Exeter on Saturday night was up there with the best of them.

Saracens at home in the Premiership, Leinster away in the Heineken Cup; those were memorable occasions.

And, this weekend, Saints wrote another impressive chapter in what has been a thrilling season so far.

Jim Mallinder's men showed immense belief to recover from 16-10 down, scoring late on through Samoan centre George Pisi to secure a 17-16 success.

It wasn't a totally new experience, with hints of the win at Wasps in December present, with Stephen Myler again slotting a critical last-gasp conversion.

Saints have eked out wins on a regular basis during this campaign, showing the confidence and composure of a champion team.

But this was on another level to most of the other 19 victories this season.

Why? Because of the level of adversity that stood in Saints' way.

They were shorn of eight international stars, while Exeter were without just one: England wing Jack Nowell.

They had injury issues during the game, with chief line-out caller and authoritative lock Christian Day limping off during the first half.

There was a swirling wind to contend with, which, as locals admitted before the game, Exeter are more than acclimatised to.

And then there was a home side baying for the blood of a team who could go top of the table with a win.

Saints stood up to it all, soaked up the punches and proved they don't have a glass jaw this season.

They have learned how to win tight games. Dare it be said – they've taken a leaf out of Leicester's book.

They now have the class and coolness to prevail in the stickiest of situations.

Even when things started to unravel during the second half, with GJ van Velze, who took over line-out calling duties from Day, in the bin, Saints refused to buckle.

They could have given Exeter another three points that would have put the home side out of sight. They didn't.

Instead, they patiently gained ground and turned on the power up front to win a string of scrum penalties close to the Chiefs line.

That gave Pisi the platform to pounce for what proved to be a telling score, with Myler easily adding the extras.

And, even when the ball was lost from the restart and Exeter mounted one final surge, Saints kept their guard up and saw the game out.

It wasn't the prettiest of wins. It was never going to be. But it's certainly one of the most satisfying successes on a long list of them so far this season.

The cloak of invincibility still sat proudly on Saints' shoulders after this scrappy success, and the feeling that this could just be a champion team in the making continued to grow, minute by minute.

There are times during a season when it is said that you just get a sense of something great, and this was one of them, because of the difficulty of the challenge Exeter posed and because of the composed way in which Saints dealt with it.

The win brought a place at the Premiership summit and it was fully deserved after they fought back and then battled to keep their lead as the Chiefs tried to rally with one last charge.

Myler had again done the business with the boot, continuing his fine campaign and enhancing his 'Iceman' reputation with another nerveless, match-winning kick.

However, this was about more than one man. It was about a team who just refused to know when they were beaten, even without the experience of their international players.

Everyone of a Saints persuasion was to enjoy their long journey back from the West Country and Mallinder was a more than happy man as he headed to conduct post-match media duties in Sandy Park's makeshift media room.

'We camped down in their 22 for the last 15 minutes, had a number of plays where we came close and to score that try with a couple of minutes to go was outstanding,' the director of rugby said.

'We talked about Exeter and how they play for 80 minutes and we would have to do the same. That's exactly how it was, to score the try with three minutes to go.

'We're in a good place at the moment. We've got internationals doing well for England and for Wales and we've got some good lads back at home.'

Exeter boss Rob Baxter felt his team had been 'passive' in defeat, but there could be no doubting that Saints' desire and ability to deal with adversity had an effect on the usually water-tight Chiefs.

The fact that the away side had scored three tries to the home side's one demonstrated which defence had come out on top and George Pisi, who grabbed that precious late five-pointer, was quick to express just what the result indicated about Saints.

'That win shows the togetherness that we have as a team,' Pisi said. 'Everyone's playing for each other and we've come a long way this season.'

Saints certainly had, but experienced campaigners such as Dowson and Wood were urging caution, despite the lofty league position, stressing nothing could be won in February and ensuring there was no chance their team-mates would let their guard down. Those messages were made more important by the two games that were to follow, with Saints huge favourites to extend their nine-match winning run, against struggling Worcester Warriors and Newcastle Falcons.

Ma'afu warned that Northampton were now there to be shot at after taking the lead at the top, but there was a welcome boost

Saints chairman Leon Barwell passed away in June 2013, but was still a big inspiration during the double-winning season

September: Ken Pisi scored as Saints got their season off to a flying start with a big win against Exeter Chiefs at Franklin's Gardens

September: Saints beat Harlequins, and the weather, to secure an impressive away win

September: Jamie Elliott scored Saints' try of the season, but it wasn't enough as Gloucester grabbed a controversial late win at Kingsholm

September: George Pisi dived over for a score as Saints cruised to victory against Sale at the Gardens

October: Tigers boss Richard Cockerill found a vantage point for the big derby match after he was hit by a ban

October: Dylan Hartley scored for Saints at Stade Pierre Antoine but Saints were beaten by Castres

October: Christian Day scored in the important Heineken Cup victory against Ospreys

October: Samu Manoa helped Saints to slay Saracens in an impressive Franklin's Gardens demolition job

November: *James Wilson was congratulated by Saints' replacements after scoring at the Madejski Stadium*

November: *Alex Day dotted down twice as the youngsters impressed against Gloucester at Franklin's Gardens*

November: Ethan Waller was on the scoresheet in a big Anglo-Welsh Cup win at London Irish

November: James Wilson scored during the second half as Saints eventually broke down a stubborn Newcastle side

November: Tom Wood registered against his former club as Saints managed to avoid a shock at Worcester

December: Calum Clark showed his disappointment after Saints were humbled at home by Leinster

December: Jamie Elliott sprinted clear to seal a stunning victory for Saints against Leinster at the Aviva Stadium

December: Stephen Myler kicked a last-gasp penalty to secure a nail-biting win against Wasps at Adams Park

December: Saints finished 2013 in style as Christian Day's double helped them to earn a resounding win against Bath

January: *A battered and bruised Dylan Hartley scored as Saints beat Harlequins at Franklin's Gardens*

January: *George North scored on the return to his homeland as Ospreys were beaten at the Liberty Stadium*

January: *George Pisi dived over for the only try of the game against Castres as Saints did enough to earn a place in the Challenge Cup*

January: *Gareth Denman waded in with a score as Saints proved to be muddy marvels at Newport*

February: Samu Manoa rubbed salt in the Saracens wounds once again with a try in the Anglo-Welsh Cup clash at Franklin's Gardens

February: Stephen Myler held his nerve to boot Saints to a last-gasp victory against Exeter at Sandy Park

February: GJ van Velze scored twice against the club he would be joining at the end of the season as Worcester were beaten at Franklin's Gardens

February: James Wilson once again showed he was the man for all seasons as he grabbed a brace on a shocking surface at Kingston Park

March: *Calum Clark grabbed a try in a comfortable win for Saints against Gloucester as the impressive unbeaten run continued*

March: *George Pisi was Saints' hat-trick hero as they saw off Saracens to secure their place in the Anglo-Welsh Cup Final*

March: *There was no happy ending in the Anglo-Welsh Cup as Exeter claimed the silverware at their Sandy Park home*

March: George North was back from international duty but Saints were beaten in the Aviva Premiership game at Sale

March: Ethan Waller scored three minutes from time but it was too little, too late as Leicester claimed a controversial win at Franklin's Gardens

April: Ben Nutley was at the double as Saints beat Sale on a Thursday night in Salford to secure a semi-final spot in the Challenge Cup

April: Saints fought back but were beaten by a narrow margin in their game against Saracens at Allianz Park

April: Salesi Ma'afu was a hugely popular scorer as Saints got a much-needed win against London Irish at Franklin's Gardens

April: Kahn Fotuali'i pulled the strings for Saints as they beat Harlequins to earn a Challenge Cup Final place

May: Jamie Elliott scored for Saints as they claimed a crucial draw in their entertaining game at Bath

May: Tom Stephenson was among the scorers as Saints crushed Wasps in the final game of the regular season

May: Salesi Ma'afu was red carded for punching Tom Youngs during the second half of a fractious derby at Franklin's Gardens

May: Tom Wood scored the winning try as Saints finally beat their rivals to set up a trip to Twickenham

May: Saints beat Bath to lift the Challenge Cup in Cardiff

May: Jim Mallinder, Tom Wood and Dylan Hartley proudly posed with the two trophies as a crowd of around 30,000 turned out to celebrate with the champions in Northampton town centre

May: Saints lifted the Premiership trophy for the first time in their history after seeing off Saracens

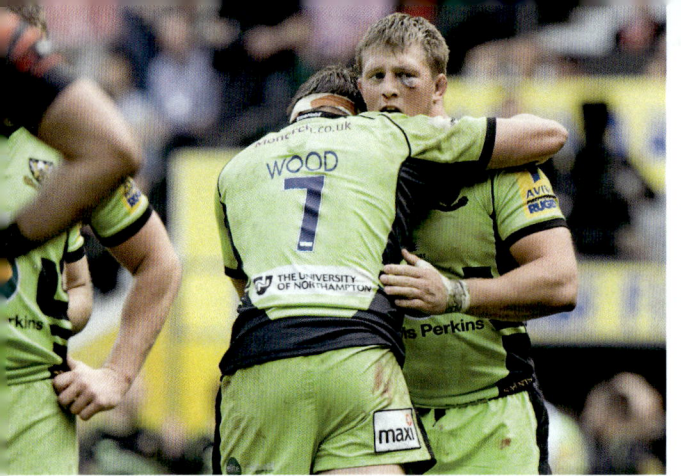

May: Alex Waller was the last-gasp hero as Saints beat Saracens

May: Luis Ghaut was the Saints mascot on Premiership Final day

May: The Saints supporters celebrated a stunning Premiership Final success at Twickenham thanks to Alex Waller's last-gasp try

May: Andy Holmes with GJ van Velze and James Wilson, who he picked up with the Premiership trophy outside McDonald's after the title celebrations went into the early hours of the following day

in the form of Lee Dickson, who returned from England duty in time for the clash with the Warriors at Franklin's Gardens.

Much of the talk in the build-up to that battle centred around the match official appointment, with Wayne Barnes taking charge of a Saints game for the first time since dismissing Hartley in the 2013 Premiership Final.

It was fair to say that he was not to be given a warm welcome in Northampton, but the team had more to think about than who the whistler was. They simply wanted another win as they sought to further banish those bad memories from the previous campaign.

Hartley would not be present as he was still with England, but Haywood's fine form was ensuring that Saints didn't suffer during the Six Nations Championship period.

Worcester were desperate for a victory in their bid to beat the drop and they headed to the Gardens buoyed by a strong display against Leicester a week earlier. The Tigers had suffered a scare at Sixways but eventually managed to run out narrow winners, leaving the Warriors with a record of 13 defeats in as many league games.

That barren run ensured that no one gave them a chance of seeing off a Saints group going in very much the opposite direction and that meant it would be a dangerous fixture.

However, the statistics didn't lie and if Saints, who had been behind at half-time in the reverse fixture earlier in the campaign, did not prevail, there would be plenty of red faces in the ranks at the Gardens.

Game 24: Saturday, 15 February 2014: Northampton Saints 30 Worcester Warriors 14 (Aviva Premiership – round 14)

Saints: Wilson; K Pisi, G Pisi (Autagavaia 71), Stephenson, Elliott; Myler (Hooley 75), L Dickson (Fotuali'i 52); A Waller (E Waller 64),

Haywood (McMillan 71), Ma'afu (Denman 53), Manoa, Dickinson, Clark (Nutley 64), Dowson (c), van Velze.

Worcester Warriors: Pennell; Drauniniu, Grove, Fatiaki, Lemi; Warwick (Mieres 60), Arr (Hodgson 69); Fainga'anuku (Porter 69), Creevy (Brooker 60), Andress (O'Donnell 64), Schofield (Percival 51), Galarza, Senatore (de Carpentier 57), Betty, Thomas.

Referee: Wayne Barnes

Attendance: 12,553

Tries: Saints: Penalty try, GJ van Velze (2). **Worcester Warriors:** David Lemi

Conversions: Saints: Stephen Myler (3)

Penalties: Saints: Stephen Myler (3). **Worcester Warriors:** Chris Pennell (3)

When a player who is third choice in his chosen position comes into the team, scores twice and picks up the man of the match award, you know you're in good shape.

That was the case for Saints on Saturday as GJ van Velze made his mark, once again demonstrating the incredible depth the squad now possesses.

In the process, he showed Worcester, the club he has agreed to join this summer, just what he is capable of.

But the crucial thing from a Northampton perspective was that once again it was a day when players stepped up and got the job done.

Van Velze can consider himself unfortunate to be in a position – at No.8 – where Sam Dickinson and Samu Manoa, in particular, have shone this season.

But when he gets a chance, the South African usually takes it. And he's not the only one.

England Under-20s centre Tom Stephenson came into the side for his first Aviva Premiership start, showcasing how bright his future promises to be.

At the other end of the experience spectrum was Lee Dickson, who returned from the England camp and looked razor sharp.

Add to that yet more positive contributions from players coming off the bench, and things are looking pretty rosy at the Gardens.

Worcester, to their credit, scrapped hard, refusing to yield territory and doing their best to cause a sizeable upset.

But they were hampered by a lack of discipline that saw Jonathan Thomas sent off for striking Sam Dickinson in the face and Leonardo Senatore and Sam Betty sin-binned.

They couldn't afford such absences on an afternoon when they were always likely to have their work cut out.

Wayne Barnes would have hoped for a quiet afternoon as he refereed a Saints game for the first time since dismissing Dylan Hartley in last May's Premiership Final. But it wasn't to be, as he dished out more cards than Casanova on Valentine's Day.

Warriors boss Dean Ryan wasn't delighted with the performance of the officials after the game, but the pressure Saints were able to build put them in a tough position.

And it cannot be denied that the best side prevailed.

Worcester did emerge with credit and their application was emphasised by a final ten minutes which saw Saints starved of the score which would have brought the bonus point.

But, as Jim Mallinder pointed out, for his team it was all about claiming another win, and Northampton remains the name at the top of the table.

It's now ten wins in a row for Mallinder's men, nine in the Aviva Premiership, which is a fine record at the best of times.

But when you consider the list of absentees currently includes Messrs Corbisiero, Hartley, Lawes, Wood, Burrell, North, Day and Foden, it's even more significant.

Fans of Saints used to look at the Six Nations Championship period with trepidation, now they view it with excitement.

It's a chance to see those players who haven't had much game time, but who can consider themselves unfortunate on that score.

Van Velze is one of those and his ability and attitude serves to illustrate the abundance of quality in the current Saints squad.

They will certainly need it if they are to maintain their current run, but this group should expect to do just that in the coming weeks.

There was a touch of inevitability about Saints' win against Worcester and you probably could have predicted which man would really make his mark against the Warriors.

Van Velze, having agreed to move to Sixways the following season, scored twice to secure a tenth successive win in all competitions on an afternoon when there were just as many cards as tries.

Barnes opted to dismiss Jonathan Thomas for punching Dickinson, leaving Warriors boss Ryan seeing red as he felt it was a 'slap' and said he had 'seen worse cuddles'. Ryan also felt Dickinson should be 'embarrassed' for going to ground, saying 'he got a slap round the face and fell over'.

It made for good entertainment in the press room, where Mallinder was taking an opposing view, backing the usually unpopular Barnes, who had sin-binned Dickinson as well as Warriors duo Sam Betty and Leonardo Senatore during the game, for his decision-making.

In truth, there was no need for Mallinder to take issue with anything because his team had won yet again and, yet again, the squad had stood up to the test against a belligerent opponent.

Things were to get even better for the club a couple of days later as Packman scored twice to help Saints secure the Under-18s league title with a final victory over Exeter Chiefs at Allianz Park.

Harry Mallinder was also among the scorers, showing just how much talent Northampton fans could look forward to seeing in years to come. However, it was still all about the short term as the bid to hold on to top spot was taken up north to Kingston Park, where another struggling side, Newcastle, lay in wait in a Sunday showdown.

Saints had relentlessly picked up what Mallinder senior described as 'bonus wins' during the Six Nations Championship and they were strongly fancied to claim another at the expense of the Falcons.

'It's not easy,' Mallinder said. 'Every point you've got to work hard for. If we can just keep winning then when the internationals come back we'll be in a very good position.'

Once again, the players were making all the right noises, with Alex Waller insisting complacency would not creep into his side's game against a team who had lost their past eight league games.

Clark was even more direct with his approach to the game, with the flanker stressing his disregard for league tables, knowing they wouldn't win the match for his team on the day.

'I don't really care a lot for league tables and form because it doesn't really owe you a lot when you're out there on the pitch,' Clark had said. 'It doesn't really stand for anything.

'Newcastle will step it up at home, I'm sure. They're coached to win those type of battles and to really test us up front so it's another week where we're going to have to do the business.'

Newcastle had proved to be a tough nut to crack on their visit to the Gardens, where Saints eventually ran out 18-0 winners thanks to two second-half tries, and there was no doubt that this was something of a free hit for the hosts.

With London Irish having shocked Saracens at Allianz Park a couple of weeks earlier, the top teams were on their guard in games against the league's strugglers.

Attack coach King urged his players to keep their discipline against a well-drilled team, but in the back of his mind, he knew it would take a huge upset for Saints to be taken out of their ever-quickening stride.

Game 25: Sunday, 23 February 2014: Newcastle Falcons 16 Northampton Saints 22 (Aviva Premiership – round 15)

Newcastle Falcons: Tait; Cato, Tiesi, Helleur (Powell 47), Shortland; Clegg (Hodgson 63), Blair (Fury 71); Vickers (Strain 15), Thompson, Tomaszczyk (Brookes 63), MacLeod, McKenzie, Wilson, Welch (c), Hogg (York 40).

Saints: Wilson; K Pisi (Autagavaia 73), G Pisi, Stephenson, Elliott; Myler, Fotuali'i; A Waller (E Waller 59), Haywood (McMillan 73), Ma'afu (Denman 59), Manoa, C Day (Nutley 64), Clark (van Velze 60), Dowson (c), Dickinson.

Referee: Andrew Small

Attendance: 4,846

Tries: Newcastle Falcons: Noah Cato. **Saints:** James Wilson (2), Tom Stephenson

Conversions: Newcastle Falcons: Joel Hodgson. **Saints:** Stephen Myler (2)

Penalties: Newcastle Falcons: Rory Clegg (3). **Saints:** Stephen Myler

---

On a surface more akin to a racecourse than a rugby pitch, Saints once again showed their pedigree to pick up another four points. At times in the second half the going was extremely heavy, but the race was already won thanks to a slick exit from the stalls.

James Wilson's double and Tom Stephenson's silky score put Saints in a position of power that they never looked likely to relinquish.

Having registered three times before the break, they may regret not grabbing all five points, but, in truth, the second half never promised to yield a fourth try.

Instead, Newcastle finally found their feet to mount a challenge, with former Saint Noah Cato's try giving them a losing bonus point.

It was one widely celebrated in the battle against the drop, with the Falcons opting to kick the ball out late on rather than go for what could have been a match-winning score.

That says a lot about their situation, and it says a lot about Saints, too.

Newcastle know all about the ability in this Northampton team and weren't prepared to gamble with their point.

They stuck instead of twisting.

For Saints, it meant another win, their tenth in succession in the Aviva Premiership and 11th in a row in all competitions.

That impressive sequence has been achieved through grit and determination in varying conditions.

There has been wind, rain and plenty of mud, but Saints have stuck to their guns and come out on top.

This game had extra demands, with a smiling Sam Dickinson revealing in his post-match interview that some of his team-mates felt like they were sinking while standing on the pitch.

Catching and kicking took on a whole new dimension as the players battled what resembled quicksand underfoot, making life pretty tricky for all concerned.

But Saints weren't about to complain, dealing with the conditions well and still managing to play plenty of rugby.

The forwards have come to the fore during the fine recent run, but the first half saw the backs also step up to the plate.

Scrum half Kahn Fotuali'i was involved in everything, fizzing the ball around the park at a speed the Falcons struggled to cope with.

Wilson popped up in all the right places and Stephenson showed he could side-step a man in a phone box as he made his way over the line.

Stephen Myler also demonstrated plenty of invention and no member of the starting 15 lacked in creativity or application.

The second half was a very different story, with the performance as turgid as the pitch.

But Saints had done what they needed to.

They'd fought the Falcons and the conditions and come out on top.

And on days like that, you have to chisel the mud off your boots and be happy with the four points.

They might not have cantered to victory, but Saints are still very much on track for claiming the grandest of national trophies at Twickenham come May.

Any Saints players wanting to discover what it would be like to be a racehorse got the chance to find out at Kingston Park as they desperately tried to plough through a surface that even the finest filly would struggle with.

Thankfully for Mallinder's men, they had all-weather ace Wilson to call upon as he scored twice, while Stephenson, who had been growing in stature during the previous few weeks, showed his fine footwork to register a try of his own in another Northampton win.

Just as in January, it was to be four wins from as many matches in February for Saints as they again allied steel with style to return home from their long trip up north with four more Premiership points in their collective pocket.

The Falcons did threaten a late comeback, but they were satisfied with a losing bonus point in the end and, in another ugly encounter, Stephenson's eye-catching try was the main talking point after the match.

'It was a great try,' Mallinder said. 'He showed really good feet on a difficult surface and he's getting better and better. We're pleased with him. He's a young Academy lad who's coming through and growing into a good Premiership player now.'

Wilson's contribution wouldn't be ignored either and he donned a broad smile as he entered the press room to discuss what was a fine personal performance.

The Kiwi's secure showing once again came in the absence of Foden, who was going to be named on the bench but Saints, having taken a look at the surface, wisely decided not to risk the full back on his return from injury.

Wilson was happy to do the business in Foden's absence and without the international players, as Saints continued to set themselves up nicely for when the Six Nations Championship reached its conclusion.

Not only was the pursuit of silverware going well, but the international stars were shining with North scoring in Wales's win against France on the same weekend as Saints beat Newcastle, and Hartley, Lawes, Wood, Burrell and Lee Dickson helping England beat Ireland.

However, while the Six Nations Championship players had no time to kick back and relax, neither did those holding the fort at Northampton with another league game, against Gloucester, just around the corner.

Dickinson stated in the aftermath of the Newcastle win that he and his team-mates were still striving to improve, and those words were certainly ominous for the teams that would be tasked with trying to stop the Saints steamroller during the month of March.

'No one rests on their laurels, especially at this time of the season when there's internationals away and there's other lads trying to take opportunities,' Dickinson said. 'It's a constant drive for improvement.'

That would be taken into the Gloucester game, but, first, there was a nice moment for the Barwell family, who saw their name put to what would be a new stand at the Gardens.

The Barwell Stand would replace the Sturtridge Pavilion and mark the immense contribution of a family who had played a key role in shaping Northampton Saints into the success story it had become.

Back on the pitch, reigning player of the year Manoa was busy stating that he felt in peak condition ahead of the visit of the Cherry and Whites, while Dowson was getting ready to celebrate a special milestone.

Having been named skipper for the Gloucester game, the influential flanker would make his 200th Premiership appearance, more than 12 years since making his league debut for former club Newcastle.

'Passing the 200-appearance milestone in the Premiership is pretty rare, and reflects Phil's consistency throughout his career,' Mallinder had said in praise of the experienced back row forward.

'He sets himself the highest standards and is a great example for the other players at the club. Phil certainly deserves all the congratulations that will come his way in the game against Gloucester.'

There was also good news for Foden as he readied himself to make his long-awaited comeback from injury, taking his place among a strong set of replacements, which also included Manoa and Lee Dickson.

Saints had been knocked off the top of the table by Saracens, who were happily picking up bonus-point wins, but they could return to the summit with a success against the Cherry and Whites.

Manoa urged his team-mates to grab revenge for their irksome defeat at Kingsholm earlier in the season, while

Mallinder heaped yet more praise on his players for the way they had been performing.

Praise and pats on the back were becoming commonplace, with winning now a habit at the Gardens, where everyone was wondering just how long this team would go without losing a game. Could a Gloucester group who liked to throw the ball about cause issues for Saints? Or would they just become the latest in a long line of victims for a team who were savagely seeing off everyone who dared to stand in their way?

Game 26: Saturday, 1 March 2014: Northampton Saints 39 Gloucester 13 (Aviva Premiership – round 16)

Saints: Wilson (Foden 51); K Pisi, G Pisi (Hooley 77), Stephenson, Elliott; Myler, Fotuali'i (L Dickson 51); E Waller (A Waller 51), Haywood (McMillan 76), Ma'afu (Mercey 53), Dickinson (Nutley 65), C Day, Clark, Dowson (c), van Velze (Manoa 33).

Gloucester: Cook; Sharples, Trinder, Tindall (c), M Thomas (Monahan 67); F Burns (B Burns 60), Robson (Knoyle 67); Y Thomas (Murphy 55), Edmonds (George 53), Harden (Puafisi 63), Stooke (James 70), Hudson, Cox, Kvesic, Evans (Moriarty 67).

Referee: Tim Wigglesworth

Attendance: 13,238

Tries: Saints: Ken Pisi, Calum Clark, Tom Stephenson, Alex Waller, Will Hooley. **Gloucester:** Henry Trinder

Conversions: Saints: Stephen Myler (4). **Gloucester:** Freddie Burns

Penalties: Saints: Stephen Myler (2). **Gloucester:** Freddie Burns (2)

The Saints players could almost have been forgiven for pulling out the party poppers as they celebrated a plethora of special landmarks in the 39-13 win against Gloucester on Saturday.

Milestone after milestone occurred in what was, eventually, another convincing victory on home turf.

There was a 200th Premiership appearance for skipper Phil Dowson, greeted with warm applause from the home fans before the game.

There was a first Premiership start for young prop Ethan Waller, who replaced brother Alex in the starting line-up.

There was a first Premiership try for flanker Calum Clark, at the 94th time of asking.

There was a first senior score for 20-year-old back Will Hooley, who grabbed his club's 50th try of the Premiership season. In just 16 games.

There were also special moments for Ken Pisi, who crowned his birthday week with a try, and Tom Stephenson, scoring for the second time in six days with another side-step try that will live long in the memory.

And then there was Ben Foden, the England full back who came off the bench to put in a sharp showing after missing the previous 13 games with a knee injury.

Fans pay money to witness pivotal moments. Moments that get them off their seats. And they certainly got their fair share on Saturday.

It was something of an 'I was there when ...' day, but it hadn't looked likely to be at half-time.

Gloucester were only three points down at the break after unwrapping a gift from Kahn Fotuali'i, whose pass was intercepted by scorer Henry Trinder.

After Pisi took advantage of a Gloucester knock-on inside the first four minutes, Saints were guilty of some uncharacteristic sloppiness. It gave the Cherry and Whites a sniff of repeating the win they secured at Kingsholm back in September.

Fotuali'i and James Wilson, probably the two most consistently impressive players during the past few weeks, both endured unusual off-days and were taken off ten minutes into the second half.

But, as has been the case so often for Saints this season, when some men aren't quite hitting their straps, others come on to lift the levels and raise the stadium roof.

The introduction of Foden and fellow England star Lee Dickson, along with Alex Waller and Tom Mercey up front, did just that.

And Gloucester, having competed so well for 55 minutes, just couldn't live with the increase in aggression and tempo.

Top teams show their class when the chips are down.

That is what Saints, the Premiership's current summit side, did.

A year ago, they lost 27-11 to Gloucester at the Gardens, presenting two tries to Jonny May on a day that proved to be the season's nadir. But this time there was to be no repeat. Trinder's try wasn't the catalyst for a home collapse.

Instead, Saints dusted themselves off, shrugged their shoulders and got on with securing yet another win.

The final 25 minutes encapsulated a 26-point spree for the home team. Gloucester didn't get anything on the board during that time.

It meant revenge for that early-season defeat at Kingsholm was served in emphatic style.

All that was lacking was the party poppers.

Revenge had been served cold at the Gardens on an afternoon when everything clicked in the second half for a Saints team who were still refusing to relent in their quest for silverware.

Everything was going right, which was a far cry from Gloucester's previous Premiership visit to the Gardens little more than a year earlier, when Mallinder's men were in a slump, desperately searching for direction.

However, they were only going in one direction at this point, and that direction was up as they again moved to the top of the

Premiership table, positioning themselves perfectly for a final push which would come after a return to LV= Cup action.

Saints had every right to believe they could win that competition thanks to the way the young men they called upon stepped up against Gloucester, with Stephenson's second eye-catching try in as many games a real highlight.

There was also a first Premiership score in Northampton colours for Clark, and Mallinder was quick to express his excitement after seeing his young guns fire again.

'The future's looking good,' said Mallinder, who was using his club's ever-improving Academy system to its full effect. 'We've won four out of four in the Premiership with the international players away and now we can move on to the LV= Cup.'

The chances of glory in that competition looked high, with a semi-final at home to Saracens beckoning on the following weekend, and Saints knew games against Gloucester usually had a catalytic effect on their fortunes.

They were desperate to maintain their momentum in the bid to reach the Sandy Park showpiece – and a win against Saracens was always welcome, no matter which competition it came in.

Mallinder would again opt to rotate, with Foden making a first start since November and a strong bench named as Manoa, Myler and Clark took their place among the replacements.

However, you got the feeling that Saints could have called a couple of fans into their starting 15 and still won, with confidence so high at the club that they almost seemed untouchable.

Saracens would, of course, be keen to upset the apple cart, but they had seen the Indian sign they once held over Saints disappear. Suddenly, Mallinder's men had got over their Sarries-shaped mental block, which had been so severe in 2012, winning their previous three meetings with the men from Barnet.

That impressive recent record was one Saints were so keen to continue, especially with the real prospect that they would meet

Saracens again in the Premiership play-offs later in the season. There was a desire to keep a foot on the throat of the title rivals, and this LV= Cup semi-final showdown provided the chance to do that, as well as setting up a trophy tilt on the weekend that would follow.

Game 27: Saturday, 8 March 2014: Northampton Saints 26 Saracens 7 (LV= Cup semi-final)

Saints: Foden; K Pisi, G Pisi, Stephenson, Collins (Autagavaia 66); Hooley (A Day 75), Fotuali'i; E Waller (A Waller 50), Haywood (McMillan 65), Mercey (Denman 60), Craig (Manoa 57), C Day, Nutley (Clark 57), Dowson (c), Dickinson.

Saracens: Ransom; Tagicakibau (Wyles 65), Streather, Bosch, Wilson; Mordt (Hodgson 57), Spencer (de Kock 57); Barrington (Gill 48), George (Saunders 75), du Plessis (Johnston 48), Sheriff (Smith 57), Botha, Melck (de Jager 57), Hankin, Wray.

Referee: Leighton Hodges

Attendance: 11,062

Tries: Saints: George Pisi (3). **Saracens:** Ben Ransom

Conversions: Saints: Stephen Myler. **Saracens:** Ben Spencer

Penalties: Saints: Will Hooley (2)

Drop goals: Saints: Stephen Myler

Whatever oranges are on offer in the Franklin's Gardens home dressing room at half-time these days, they're clearly working.

Because the transformation from first to second half has been quite striking in the past couple of weeks.

On Saturday, Saints overcame a first 40 minutes in which they had minimal possession of the ball, to see off Saracens in emphatic fashion. George Pisi's second-half hat-trick slayed the Allianz Park outfit and set up a place in next Sunday's Sandy Park LV= Cup Final against Exeter Chiefs.

But it wasn't simply about the Samoan, as the man himself was keen to point out in his post-match interview.

This was a team who went from Hyde to Jekyll in little more than a half-time break and a few second-half minutes.

It was a similar scenario to last weekend, when Saints were locked at 13-13 with Gloucester before pulling away in the final 25 minutes.

They have taken their time to get up and running, but once they click into gear it has devastating effects.

Everything about the final stages of Saturday's performance was quicker, slicker and more ruthless.

There was a Polynesian flavour to all three tries as George Pisi applied the finishing touches, with brother Ken and scrum half Kahn Fotuali'i also hugely influential.

As always, the pack played a huge part, with the likes of Alex Waller and Samu Manoa again coming off the bench to add extra bite.

Saracens, so in control of proceedings for the final 30 minutes of the first half, were suddenly struggling to stem the tide.

And they were made to pay for not making the most of the stranglehold on proceedings they seemed to have at one point.

Marcelo Bosch's disallowed try was, as both bosses later admitted, something of a game-changer, as Saints finally got their act together.

And they can now look forward to an 80-minute shot at the silverware at Sandy Park next Sunday.

For Saracens, who were taunted with chants of 'Can we play you every week?' by the Saints faithful at the end, it was an opportunity lost.

They have now lost their past four games against Jim Mallinder's men, who will hope that can give them a mental edge should they meet in the Premiership play-offs.

For now, though, it's all about the LV= Cup Final for Saints.

They'd just better remember to transport those oranges down to Exeter next weekend.

The chants that rang around Franklin's Gardens towards the end of this game were music to the ears of Saints, who had managed to maintain their sensational winning run while putting another knife in Saracens' season.

The cries of 'Can we play you every week?' would have hurt Saracens, but for Saints it was so sweet as they set up another LV= Cup Final appearance with a comprehensive second-half showing.

Mallinder's plan to bring power off the bench worked to perfection as George Pisi showed his finishing prowess with a hat-trick.

Again, the winning mentality that was embedded in the team came to the fore as, just as they had against Gloucester, Saints overcame some sticky moments early on to get the result they wanted.

As mentioned before, they had forgotten what it was like to lose, while Saracens were starting to forget what it was like to beat a Northampton team.

'It's a nice place to be, winning games,' said the typically understated Mallinder. 'Momentum is important and it gives you belief. The lads have got that at the moment, they know how to win games.

'We were under the cosh at times against Saracens, so it was brilliant to see the players come out and believe they could win, and ultimately do that.'

Mallinder did admit his men had ridden their luck at times, with Saracens having gone 7-6 up before seeing a Marcelo Bosch try disallowed, but the director of rugby stressed his delight at how his team had managed to weather the storm to secure the victory.

Mallinder's opposite number, Mark McCall, admitted Saints had simply been too clinical for his team, who saw their LV= Cup hopes go up in smoke.

It would be Saints who would travel to Sandy Park on the following Sunday, when Exeter Chiefs would provide the opposition as the West Country side sought to claim glory on home soil. Mental strength was something Saints had plenty of, and they would need it in the build-up to the final, with the coaches telling their players not to be fazed by the fact the Chiefs would hold home advantage.

Saints had already conquered Sandy Park once during the campaign, with that nail-biting Premiership victory a month earlier still fresh in the memory, though Dowson was quick to play down the significance of it going into the game.

'This is a completely different entity,' said Dowson, who had captained Saints to LV= Cup glory at Sixways in March 2010. 'They're at home and in a final and the games beforehand don't really have much of a say.

'We need to make sure we learned the lessons from last time, but it doesn't give us any advantage having played there recently.'

You always felt the messages may have been slightly different in the dressing room, with mentions of that Sandy Park success surely used as a reason to be confident against a team who had plenty of belief of their own.

Exeter had become a formidable force, especially at home, and Saints would need another special display if they were to extend their 13-match winning streak and take the silverware home.

It was another week full of tough selection decisions for Mallinder, who was still missing his England men. The national team had won against Wales on the previous Sunday and were busy setting their sights on Italy on the same weekend as the LV= Cup Final.

146

Saints knew that winning the competition would be the perfect way to cap a period in which their squad had shown its immense strength in the absence of some of its biggest stars.

However, the Chiefs, a team who prided themselves on team ethic rather than individuals, would certainly not be an easy bunch to push over in what promised to be a gargantuan battle for the season's first piece of silverware.

Game 28: Sunday, 16 March 2014: Exeter Chiefs 15 Northampton Saints 8 (LV= Cup Final)

Exeter Chiefs: Arscott; Vainikolo, Dollman, Shoemark, Jess; Slade, Lewis; Moon, Whitehead (Cowan-Dickie 66), Tui (Brown 66); Mumm, Welch; Ewers, White (Armand 50), Horstmann.

Saints: Foden; K Pisi, G Pisi, Wilson, Elliott; G Dickson (A Day 74), Fotuali'i; A Waller (E Waller 64), Haywood, Ma'afu (Mercey 49), Manoa, Day, Clark (Nutley 50), Dowson, van Velze.

Referee: Andrew Small

Attendance: 10,004

Tries: Exeter Chiefs: Chris Whitehead, Dean Mumm. **Saints:** Samu Manoa

Conversions: Exeter Chiefs: Henry Slade

Penalties: Exeter Chiefs: Henry Slade. **Saints:** Glenn Dickson

---

After most supporters had exited Sandy Park, Rob Baxter made his way up the steps of the main stand.

The Exeter Chiefs boss, can of Heineken in hand, was greeted with a hero's welcome by friends and family.

It was an interesting sight, as just five weeks earlier, Saints boss Jim Mallinder had been the man receiving the plaudits in the same corner of the West Country ground.

Mallinder had masterminded a late Aviva Premiership success in atrocious conditions, keeping an impressive run going with the international players away. The men who remained at the club kept their cool and composure in the face of a blue tide of Chiefs defence, eventually breaking through to score a third, match-winning try late on.

This time, though, there was to be no repeat.

Instead, Exeter stood firm, despite Samu Manoa scoring in the same corner as he had in the meeting last month.

That proved to be too little, too late for Saints, who, on this occasion, gave themselves too much to do.

They had been made to pay for some poor handling and a failure to do the basics right as the Chiefs gave them a taste of their own medicine.

It was hard to swallow and although every team can have an off day – heck, it's almost expected when you've won 13 games on the bounce – Saints may just be left feeling they didn't do themselves justice.

It was a fourth final defeat in as many years, but of those this was the one they had the most momentum and expectation going into.

Exeter had home advantage, and it did make a difference as they lifted their levels beyond the norm, but a Saints team in top form would have secured the silverware.

The result was what happens when the team who are given the favourites' tag play below their capabilities against a plucky underdog playing to their full potential.

It was to be another tough experience as the trophy was handed out and Saints were again forced to watch on as a team danced on their dreams.

But though the performance wasn't the best and the LV= Cup won't be heading back to Northampton, a little perspective must be brought to the occasion.

It was a great triumph for Exeter, the greatest in their 143-year history, but for Saints it was not the be all and end all.

They are still fighting on two fronts – with key men now back following the conclusion of the Six Nations Championship – and one of those is the one they really want, the Aviva Premiership.

Of course they wanted the LV= Cup, too.

It just so happens they met a side who wanted it more than anything they have ever wanted before.

Now it's time to refocus in pursuit of the one Saints have a similar feeling about.

The Amlin Challenge Cup is a nice side dish, but make no mistake, a first league crown is what Mallinder and his men crave the most.

This loss has reaffirmed the importance of home advantage, giving them an extra push to ensure that play-off semi-final is booked at the Gardens as soon as possible. If Saints can do that, and turn up on the big occasions in May, it will be Mallinder who is afforded the biggest hero's welcome of them all.

After 13 weeks of executing their plans to perfection, not much went right for Saints at Sandy Park.

A difficult day had begun with injury woe as not one, but two fly halves were forced to sit out the final.

Myler was due to start, but was forced to miss out with a hamstring problem, while Hooley, who was due to be his replacement, was also sidelined with a head injury.

That meant Glenn Dickson was thrust into the limelight, with Olver on the bench, and, though Dickson did little wrong, Saints were unsurprisingly affected by the fact that Myler, the fulcrum of their team, was unavailable.

Exeter exerted control on the game, suffocating Saints with their high defensive line and scoring the two tries they needed to pick up an historic win at their own ground.

Manoa did score late on for Saints, but, once again, they were forced to walk past a trophy rather than picking it up.

It was getting to the point where finals were becoming a curse, with four successive chances to lift silverware now squandered.

The Heineken Cup loss to Leinster, the Premiership defeat to Leicester, an LV= Cup reverse, also against the Tigers, and now this. There was only so long Saints could keep saying that they would learn from final disappointments.

However, they simply had to after this, with two trophies, including the big one, the Premiership, still up for grabs. A tough run of games would lie in wait, but Mallinder was determined to remain upbeat as he conducted his post-match interview on the pitch. He knew there would be bigger battles during the season and he knew that he had the squad to win them.

'It's a one-off game we've lost, but we'll be back,' Mallinder said. 'Hopefully this season we'll get to more finals and hopefully we can get that silverware that we're all looking for.'

Saints needed to shrug off their Sandy Park heartache quickly, with a trip to unhappy hunting ground Sale beckoning, but they would at least be able to look forward to welcoming back their international players during the week.

One man going in the opposite direction was Manoa as he headed off to represent the USA and there were soon decisions to be made as to how many of the men who had been involved in the Six Nations Championship – which was won by Ireland – would be parachuted straight back into life at Northampton.

The competition for places was suddenly far more intense, but it was exactly what Saints needed as they looked to bounce back from that rare defeat.

Mallinder stressed the importance of securing a top two spot and a home play-off semi-final in the Premiership, but he was well aware of the difficulty of the run of games ahead, with the match at Sale followed by an East Midlands derby against Leicester and another instalment of the Saracens rivalry.

Saints were sitting pretty at the top of the Premiership with just six games to go, but Sale would threaten that standing, with the Sharks a team on the up.

'They have improved and you've only got to see their performances,' said Mallinder. 'The interesting thing will be to see whether a little bit of rest during the recent LV= Cup weeks has been good or bad for them. You don't quite know.

'They've had three weeks off over this LV= Cup period so they've had that time without a game but I'm sure they'll be fresh and raring to get stuck into us.'

Saints certainly knew what was in store, but dealing with it would be another matter. Their 11-match Premiership winning streak was in danger and the Sharks were circling, smelling blood after seeing Exeter lift the cloak of invincibility six days earlier.

Game 29: Saturday, 22 March 2014: Sale Sharks 19 Northampton Saints 6 (Aviva Premiership – round 17)

Sale: Arscott; Brady, Leota, Tuitupou, Cueto; Cipriani, Peel (Cliff 71); Lewis-Roberts (Harrison 65), Jones, Cobillas (Thomas 66), Mills (Ostrikov 48), Paterson, Braid (c), Seymour, Gaskell.

Saints: Foden; Elliott, Wilson (G Pisi 49), Burrell, North; Hooley, L Dickson (Fotuali'i 49); A Waller, Hartley (c), Ma'afu (Mercey 50), Lawes, C Day, Clark (Dowson 49), Wood, van Velze.

Referee: Luke Pearce

Attendance: 5,428

Tries: Sale Sharks: Mark Cueto, Marc Jones, Tom Brady

Conversions: Sale Sharks: Danny Cipriani (2)

Penalties: Saints: Will Hooley (2)

There was a distracting sense of déjà vu when the final whistle blew at the AJ Bell Stadium on Saturday afternoon.

151

A palpable sense of regret filled the air as Saints trudged off the pitch to a chorus of cheers from the home fans.

It was an all too familiar scene, with memories of the LV= Cup defeat at Exeter six days earlier still fresh in the mind.

On that occasion, down at Sandy Park, the Chiefs supporters partied like it was 1999, saluting their team for slaying the Saints.

Exeter had got their noses ahead early on and never looked back, putting the squeeze on to secure the biggest result in their 143-year existence.

On Saturday, history repeated itself, as Saints suffered a similar fate against another phalanx of fired-up players, celebrating their most sizeable success of the season.

All the pre-match talk in the home camp had been about a great campaign, but one which had yet to encompass a win against one of the league's top four.

That was rectified at Saints' expense, but, just as at Exeter on the previous weekend, there was reason to feel it shouldn't have reached such a disappointing denouement.

Saints dominated possession in an entirely one-sided second half, pouring forward in pursuit of a passage back into the game.

But, with a 13-point advantage secured during a clinical first-half showing, the Sharks stood their ground, plugging gaps and routinely slowing down Saints ball.

In his pre-match interview, full back Ben Foden admitted other sides may have seen Exeter as an example. They may have seen how the Chiefs played against Saints and copied it.

And that may well have been the case for Sale, as they, like the Chiefs, showed a ruthless streak to take their chances before clinging on for dear life.

They, like the Chiefs, pushed Saints over with an inexorable maul and they, like the Chiefs, displayed a razor-sharp counter-attacking game.

They, like the Chiefs, poured everything they had into the game, upping the ante in the aggression stakes and giving Jim Mallinder's men a mountain to climb.

This Saints team is comfortable in so many situations, as shown by their recent incredible 13-match winning streak, but recovering from a sizeable deficit isn't always one of them.

Sometimes panic sets in, as it did against Leinster at Franklin's Gardens in December, with the team forcing things rather than sticking to their systems.

The lack of a plan B has also been discussed and, perhaps, Saints are occasionally guilty of trucking it up the middle a bit too often.

But what must be remembered is that their style has worked far more often than not this season. The record still reads 23 wins from 29 games, remember.

There is no reason to throw the baby out with the bathwater. Subtle adjustments should be the order of the day, not wholesale panic and knee-jerk reactions.

And the team have to be given time to get to know each other again.

Combinations are so important and, during the past couple of weeks, with key players returning, there has been plenty of chopping and changing.

Regular fly half and the man expected to set the tone, Stephen Myler, has been missing, though it has to be said his deputies have done an admirable job.

Then there are the Six Nations Championship stars, who Sale boss Steve Diamond claimed were overcome by lassitude on Saturday. You could say Saints shouldn't have thrown all of them back into the mix straight away – 'give them the weekend off', some said – but they need to be reintegrated at some point.

If not at Sale, then when? Against Leicester on Saturday? That would hardly have been ideal, either.

And as Mallinder pointed out after the game, you simply have to pick the best players you can to win the game.

Leave out the likes of Luther Burrell, George North and Dylan Hartley, lose and questions will be asked.

Pick them, lose and questions will still be asked. Put simply, selecting a side is not an exact science.

Harlequins rested their England trio against Saracens and got soundly beaten, leaving themselves with the toughest of tasks to make the play-offs.

They may be fresher for next week, but Quins may win and still be several points adrift of the top four. Saints wanted to get another victory to retain the breathing space they had built up during an impressive first 16 league games.

They didn't manage to do it, and they have held their hands up, as they did at Exeter.

But the time for accusations is over and a win against Leicester this Saturday will go a long way to banishing recollections of a frustrating couple of weeks.

'Knackered' – that was how Steve Diamond described Saints' international stars after they made an unsuccessful return to life at their club.

All six of the Six Nations Championship players were brought back in by Mallinder, but there was little cohesion and even less threat as the defeat at Exeter was exacerbated by the Premiership winning run coming to an end.

England hooker Hartley was sin-binned during the first half and things weren't to get much better as the Sharks secured their tenth league win of the campaign, leaving toothless Saints feeling flat after only having two Hooley penalties to show for their efforts.

'We looked like a side who have not played together for the last eight weeks,' Mallinder said.

However, what Mallinder was not prepared to admit was that a post-Six Nations Championship malaise was to blame for the poor performance.

'I don't think it's fitness because those lads are fit lads,' he said, responding to Diamond's criticism. 'We just couldn't string anything together. It was teamwork that let us down, not fitness.'

Whatever it was, Saints knew they had to get back in the groove quickly because the game at the Sharks would be followed by another sink or swim situation in the form of a big East Midlands derby at the Gardens on the following Saturday.

Mallinder stressed that his men would perform far better against their rivals than they had against Sale, but there was a bit of news that soured the pre-match preparations, and it came in the form of the referee appointment.

Barnes would be the man to take charge of the derby, leaving Saints fans frothing at the mouth on social media as they feared more controversial decisions from the referee who had dismissed Hartley during the previous season's Premiership Final clash with Tigers.

Not only that, but the history Barnes had in East Midlands derbies made everyone at Northampton uneasy and it was an unwanted talking point in the build-up to a match that was important in the pursuit of a home play-off semi-final.

Nevertheless, Saints vowed to focus on themselves rather than things that were out of their control and there was a desire to 'get back on the same page' after the patchy performance at Sale.

'We've got five games, we're up in a very strong position and it's down to us to bounce back,' Mallinder said. 'The game against Leicester will bring the best out of everyone.

'We are disappointed about the Sale result, but we have to put it behind us and work hard at gelling as a team. That's the secret for us. If we do that then we have the players to win.'

However, recent history was not on Saints' side as they were going into the game without a win against Tigers since September 2010. Cockerill's side had eviscerated Exeter 45-15 at Welford Road on the previous weekend and appeared to be coming into the derby in much better shape than Saints.

The messages coming from the Saints camp were, as expected, positive, with Wood, King and van Velze all taking on media duties and expressing their confidence that this was the time the Tigers would be tamed. Saints were determined to end March in style, having started it so well but faded slightly, and there would be no better way to go into April than to steamroller the irksome club from up the M1.

Game 30: Saturday, 29 March 2014: Northampton Saints 16 Leicester Tigers 22 (Aviva Premiership – round 18)

Saints: Foden; Elliott (L Dickson 65), G Pisi (K Pisi 68), Burrell, North; Hooley (Wilson 60), Fotuali'i; A Waller (E Waller 62), Hartley (Haywood 33), Ma'afu (Mercey 37), Lawes, C Day, Clark (van Velze 66), Dowson, Wood.

Leicester: Hamilton; Goneva, Tuilagi, Allen, Thompstone (Harrison 76); Williams (Flood 73), B Youngs; Ayerza, T Youngs, Mulipola (Balmain 76), Deacon (Kitchener 65), Slater (c), Gibson, Salvi, Crane.

Referee: Wayne Barnes

Attendance: 13,459

Tries: Saints: Kahn Fotuali'i, Ethan Waller. **Leicester Tigers:** Anthony Allen

Conversions: Leicester Tigers: Owen Williams

Penalties: Saints: Will Hooley, James Wilson. **Leicester Tigers:** Owen Williams (5)

Another East Midlands derby, another redefinition of the word controversy and, most importantly, another winless afternoon for Saints. Fans of the green, black and gold had every reason to believe that this would be the day they finally smashed the Leicester Tigers hoodoo to pieces.

That this time, it would be they who marched into work on Monday with smiles on their faces.

But, once again, it was those pesky Tigers who prevailed to pick up the points and the bragging rights.

It felt like Groundhog Day for Saints, with whistler Wayne Barnes in the middle of a maelstrom of contention at the end of another fractious afternoon.

So irked were Saints with the official's decision to call time when it was felt there were still a few seconds to play, that Jim Mallinder pursued him to seek clarification.

It is not something you would normally see from the typically calm and collected director of rugby, but it reflected the stresses and strains of another frustrating afternoon.

Saints have now failed to get one over on their nearest, but far from dearest, neighbours in ten meetings and there can be no doubt that this is no longer simply about ability.

It is about mentality, and the most worrying thing about everything that happened on Saturday was the consequence of the result.

Leicester's win ensured they remain on a collision course with Saints in the end-of-season play-offs – and that cannot be viewed as good news.

Richard Cockerill's men are far from invincible, particularly this season, but that is not the salient point.

The line between winning and losing big games is so fine that mentality is what tips the balance in one team's favour.

Saints used that to great effect last season as they steamrolled Saracens in the play-off semi-final at Allianz Park.

They used criticism of their failure to beat any of that season's top four to fuel their bid.

And after turning the tables, they now have the Indian sign over the men from Barnet, who have not won any of the past four meetings between the teams.

But Leicester's grip on Saints is even stronger. It's a chokehold.

Blame Barnes, blame missed kicks (Saints failed with four attempts) or blame something else, but Northampton's biggest problem was the first 35 minutes on Saturday.

They simply didn't emerge with the belief they needed, failing to exit their own half as Leicester bossed the territory and possession to fly into a 13-3 lead.

It's a long way back from there against any team, and Saints just had a bit too much to do.

Yes, they could have won it had young fly half Will Hooley kicked his goals or Barnes allowed more time at the denouement, but they shouldn't have been in that situation.

When Saints last beat Leicester, Stephen Myler – who is undoubtedly a huge miss at the moment, having been absent for the past three games – left 18 points on the field.

On that day back in September 2010, Leicester, as they are now, were reigning champions, but so comprehensive was the nature of the Northampton display that they had no answer.

Saints have put teams away left, right and centre at Franklin's Gardens, winning their previous eight league games and scoring an average of 33 points.

Leicester are no better than Saracens or Bath. But what they have that the others didn't is that mental edge.

It must also be said that Myler and reigning player of the season Samu Manoa are being missed massively. And their absence played its part, too.

But Leicester were also without a laundry list of key men and yet they still retained their unbeaten run.

Somehow, Saints are going to have to find a way to beat their rivals if they want to win the league this season.

But that is not the immediate concern.

Now it's about a final four league games in the bid to ensure Leicester don't close the seven-point gap between second and third to book themselves a home semi-final against Saints.

That would be an even greater obstacle as, despite coming close back in October, no Northampton team has won at Welford Road since 2007.

Wherever you look there are damning statistics.

But those haunting reminders won't decide the destiny of the title. Performances in May will.

And Saints must remember that when they have scratched the Leicester surface this season, they have got rewards.

The problem was that they lacked the necessary sharpness in the formative stage of Saturday's game.

Another East Midlands derby, another controversial moment and, most disappointingly for Saints, another defeat to Leicester Tigers.

All of those bullish pre-match words faded into the Franklin's Gardens air as Owen Williams kicked five penalties and converted Anthony Allen's try to help secure yet another Leicester success against Northampton.

Saints, who were still missing Myler through injury and Manoa to international duty, seemed to have the belief to get the job done, but again Leicester had more mental power and again that man Barnes came to the fore as the match descended into chaos.

The referee was followed down the tunnel by an irate Mallinder, who felt his team had enough time to take a late line-out. Barnes deemed the clock was dead and that left Saints without a chance to attempt to win the game, with the official being roundly booed as Dowson tried to stop Mallinder getting to the man in yellow.

It was another East Midlands derby full of contentious decisions and one that saw Saints stumble against the Tigers again, stretching that unwanted winless run in these clashes and making it three successive defeats in all competitions.

There was tension in the press room after the match with so much to discuss with both bosses. Mallinder was still angry as he began to answer questions, with his attention unsurprisingly focused on a certain Gloucestershire official.

'Wayne just told me afterwards that he was told the game was over,' Mallinder said. 'I don't quite know who told him that. He's in charge. We were disappointed with that. There was time on the clock.

'Their physio got his hands on the ball and Ben Foden managed to get the ball off him and there was still time on the clock. We were pretty disappointed, 15 against 13, not to have a line-out close to their line.'

Pretty disappointed was a clear understatement, while pretty chuffed didn't begin to describe Cockerill, who had once again seen his men win the derby day battle and who felt they fully deserved their triumph.

If seeing Cockerill and Tigers celebrating again on their own ground hurt, that pain was accentuated by an injury to Hartley, who was to face a fight to save his season after injuring his shoulder during a first-half ruck in the derby.

Saints would head to Sale for the Amlin Challenge Cup tie on the following Thursday without their captain and their other international stars as they used the European encounter as a chance to rest some weary bodies.

There would be no Diamond accusations of tiredness on this occasion as Mallinder named a young and enthusiastic squad for the trip up north, which hardly caught the attention due to the nature of the competition and the fact the match was not being played on a weekend.

However, Saints still wanted to get the job done and they really needed to get some momentum back during the month of April after a late-March malaise.

Dowson urged his team-mates to stick together during their winless run, just as they had done during the 13-match winning streak that preceded it. However, words were worthless. The team needed to stand up and deliver on a gloomy night at the AJ Bell Stadium to keep the European flame burning and make sure the season didn't peter out at a critical moment.

Game 31: Thursday, 3 April 2014: Sale Sharks 14 Northampton Saints 28 (Amlin Challenge Cup quarter-final)

Sale Sharks: Arscott; Brady (Mackenzie 54), Forsyth, Jennings, Miller; Macleod (Ford 60), Cliff (Fowles 50); Harrison (Croall 70), Taylor, Thomas (Buckley 60), Ostrikov, Kulemin, Gaskell (c), Easter, Fihaki.

Saints: Foden; K Pisi, Wilson (Fotuali'i 71), Stephenson (Waldouck 43 (Elliott 48)), Autagavaia; Hooley, L Dickson; E Waller (Hobbs-Awoyemi 65), McMillan (Williams 65), Mercey (Denman 43), Dickinson, Craig, Dowson (c), Nutley (Harrison 58), van Velze.

Referee: Romain Poite (France)

Attendance: 4,650

Tries: Sale Sharks: Henry Thomas, Viliami Fihaki. **Saints:** Ben Nutley, Sam Dickinson, Ben Foden, Ben Nutley

Conversions: Sale Sharks: Nick Macleod, Joe Ford. **Saints:** Will Hooley (4)

It might have been a tie that had all the glitz and glamour of dinner at a motorway service station, but Saints didn't waste the chance to fill their bellies at Sale.

Their young guns were hungry and their experienced players oozed class as the Sharks were dismissed in ruthless fashion.

And though the Amlin Challenge Cup will continue to be the season's secondary aim, with Aviva Premiership glory the priority, there is no doubt this felt good for the men in green, black and gold.

With both sides having made a host of changes – Saints changed 12 from the defeat to Leicester last weekend – it was Northampton's squad depth that once again shone through.

Time and time again, Jim Mallinder's men have flashed their blade in cup action this season, with the LV= Cup campaign – the final defeat to Exeter aside – illustrating their power in reserve.

And this was a night when Mallinder once again concocted a potent blend.

From the forwards through to the backs, Saints had exactly the right balance. And Sale simply had no answer.

Apart from one early foray that resulted in a try, the Sharks were under the cosh from minute one, drowning in a sea of Saints bodies.

The platform, as ever, was laid by the forwards, with Ethan Waller making mincemeat of England tighthead Henry Thomas, who paid the price in the form of a yellow card.

Ben Nutley, as he has done whenever he has been given an opportunity for Saints, also shone, picking up two tries for his considerable efforts, which saw him dominate at the breakdown.

And the backs made sure their contribution wouldn't be forgotten as four of them teamed up to score one of the best tries you'll see this season.

Lee Dickson's pass to Ken Pisi was sublime, Pisi's chip and gather was impressive and Will Hooley's grubber kick through for Ben Foden was a masterclass in fly half play.

It lit up the AJ Bell Stadium encounter, with the hardy bunch of Saints fans celebrating loudly as they won the battle in the stands as comprehensively as their team had done on the pitch.

The club now has another semi-final to look forward to, meaning they will have made the final four in three separate competitions this season, presuming they finish in the Premiership top four.

They have got that far because of the abundance of quality they possess through their squad, while Sale, as admitted by Steve Diamond, do not have anywhere near as much heavy artillery to call on.

It will be criminal if this Saints squad don't get at least some reward in the form of silverware for their efforts during this campaign.

They must still prove they can cut the mustard in finals, but they must get there first.

And they went exactly the right way about it as they emerged from the Salford smog with the sweet taste of success in their mouths on Thursday night.

You might not think there would be much satisfaction to be had from spending a Thursday night at a sparsely-populated stadium in Salford, but this was a very rewarding evening for Saints.

They took the opportunity to rest some key men, bringing in some young guns who were champing at the bit to propel their team into the final four in Europe.

Those players certainly took their chance, with Ethan Waller and Nutley leading the way on a night when Sale never threatened to inflict the damage they had in the Premiership meeting a couple of weeks earlier.

'It was a good first half and we learned a few lessons from two weeks ago when we lost here in the Premiership,' Mallinder said. 'We scored some good tries.

'We're delighted because it's a tough place to come on a Thursday night in particular.

'We played a number of the younger lads and they were really good. They brought some really good energy and enthusiasm to the team. It's good to get back to winning ways.'

Saints had needed this shot in the arm and after battling to victory at the AJ Bell Stadium, they set their sights on a warm weather trip to Lanzarote, which would be used to further recharge the batteries ahead of the following weekend's trip to Saracens.

'We're taking the lads away and we're going to get some serious training in out there,' said Mallinder, with tongue firmly in cheek. 'We've got a big week with Saracens away and that's going to be massive for us.

'We'll take the squad away and it's nice to go away on the back of a win as opposed to a loss.'

With a ten-day break between games, it was also the perfect time for Myler to get back on his feet after a frustrating four-game spell on the sidelines, during which Saints had won just once.

The return of the fly half, one of the campaign's stand-out players so far, would be a huge boost for the club as plans were formulated for a strong finish to the season.

Glenn Dickson and Hooley had definitely not disgraced themselves while standing in for Myler, but he had become such an integral part of the starting 15, steering the side around with aplomb and ending years of inconsistency that came with players failing to make the No.10 shirt their own.

Corbisiero was another man on the comeback trail, while Manoa had returned from international duty and Saints were starting to get their squad together for the final push, which included a Challenge Cup semi-final against Harlequins as well as the four remaining regular-season league matches.

The trip to Saracens was a big one as Saints looked to maintain their stranglehold over their Barnet-based rivals –

Mallinder's men had won their previous four games against Mark McCall's team – as well as ensure that the run of back-to-back league defeats would come to an end.

Clark called on his team-mates to reproduce their Allianz Park heroics of the previous season's play-off semi-final, while former Scarlets star North was busy setting his sights on silverware, stressing how much it meant for him to be involved in a trophy hunt with his club.

'I haven't had any experience of getting to the latter stages with the club so I'm really enjoying what is to come and the challenges that are ahead,' North said.

'As a squad, we're looking pretty good right now. We're in one piece, we've got a lot of strength in depth, we've got a lot of freshness from the young boys coming through now, pushing us on. It's a good place to be and I'm excited for the final weeks. It's going to be a big push now to finish.'

Saints needed to beat Saracens to keep pace at the top. They were desperate to secure a home play-off semi-final as opposed to plunging themselves into another away draw in the final four.

A win at Saracens would go a long way to helping them achieve their league aims, but there could be no doubt that the men dressed in the Dennis the Menace-style home shirts would have their gnashers out in the bid to bite Saints' chance of a top-two finish.

The two teams had enjoyed very different build-ups to the game, with Saints having a sojourn in Spain while Saracens were involved in a bruising Heineken Cup quarter-final in Belfast, where they beat Ulster to progress to the semi-finals.

How much had the hard work they put in taken out of them? Would Saints reap the benefits of their late-season break? And which team was better prepared as the race for the title intensified once more? As Mallinder's men marched to Barnet again, some big questions were about to be answered.

Game 32: Sunday, 13 April 2014: Saracens 28 Northampton Saints 24 (Aviva Premiership – round 19)

Saracens: Wyles; Ashton, Bosch (Streather 72), Barritt, Strettle; Farrell (Hodgson 40), de Kock (Wigglesworth 50); M Vunipola, Brits (George 50), Johnston (Stevens 50), Borthwick (c), Botha, Wray (Burger 72), Brown, B Vunipola.

Saints: Foden; Elliott, G Pisi (Wilson 70), Burrell, North; Myler, L Dickson (Fotuali'i 53); A Waller (E Waller 55), McMillan (Haywood 53), Ma'afu (Denman 55), Lawes, C Day (Dickinson 55), Clark, Wood (c), Manoa.

Referee: Matthew Carley

Attendance: 9,999

Tries: Saracens: David Strettle, Kelly Brown, Marcelo Bosch. **Saints:** Penalty try, Luther Burrell, George North

Conversions: Saracens: Owen Farrell, Charlie Hodgson. **Saints:** Stephen Myler (3)

Penalties: Saracens: Marcelo Bosch (2), Owen Farrell. **Saints:** Stephen Myler

On the day of the London Marathon, Saints were once again reminded that a season is far from a sprint.

Having won 11 league games on the spin before that run ended at Sale at the end of March, Jim Mallinder's men have now stumbled a little, suffering three successive league defeats.

Put it down to what you will, but they will be disappointed to have only taken two points from those games.

However, perspective must be applied in that the teams they have been beaten by are teak-tough. Some of the Premiership's steeliest, in fact.

Had Saints suffered losses to the likes of Worcester and Newcastle in their recent malaise, it would be easier to fire criticism their way.

But there is little shame in losing to the sides they have of late.

It's just that a run of 13 successive wins in all competitions before the LV= Cup Final defeat at Exeter set the bar so high.

As Tom Wood pointed out afterwards, they have almost been victims of their own success.

But the straight-talking England flanker was also keen not to make excuses – and there can be no doubt that Saints would have expected more from themselves on Sunday.

Against Leicester and Saracens they have paid the price for not exiting their own half effectively, inviting pressure from sides who know how to make the most of it.

Some early box-kicking continually handed the ball back to Sarries at Allianz Park and that kept them on the front foot for long periods.

Saints' discipline was also way off what it should have been, with a string of penalties proving costly.

Saracens were even able to miss a few kicks and still get home. And it was all so different to the events of last May when Saints stormed Allianz Park to record a memorable victory.

On that day, particularly in the first half, they were almost blemish-free.

They applied early pressure and forced Saracens back with waves of physicality, earning a 17-0 half-time lead before eventually going on to win 27-13.

Saracens have clearly learned from that chastening experience – and the three further sobering defeats to Saints since. This time, they soaked up monster hits from the likes of Courtney Lawes and Samu Manoa and sprung back to their feet to turn the screw.

It was impressive from the home side, who are now all but assured of a home semi-final and who will almost certainly top the regular-season table.

For Saints, there is far less security.

They can now feel the breath of Leicester Tigers on their collective neck, with just three points separating the teams with three games to go.

With the fixtures both sides have left, you'd have to fancy Saints to stay put in the top two, though recent weeks have cast some doubt over that.

What is important now is regrouping and trying to build some momentum going into May, because the race is far from run and a sprint finish lies in wait.

Saints just need to make sure they have enough left in their legs and retain the belief that they can cross the finish line with their heads held high.

As it turned out, Saracens responded to all of the questions asked of them, leaving Saints searching for answers as they sought to get their league season back on track.

This was their third successive defeat in the Premiership and while Saracens proved they could overcome their Saints hoodoo, Mallinder's men had plenty to do to show they could challenge McCall's side for the title.

With games against London Irish, Bath and Wasps still to play, there was plenty of hope that Saints could hold off the challenge of Leicester, who were now hunting them down in the bid to secure second spot and a home play-off semi-final.

However, the pressure was now being ramped up and supporters were left fearing the worst, having seen their side run out of steam to ruin trophy tilts in seasons gone by.

Would Saints stumble when it mattered again or did this team have the skill and character to negotiate a tricky situation and return to the path that would guide them towards silverware?

They had played well in patches in the game at Allianz Park and the fighting spirit they showed to get back in the game at least provided some momentum and a positive to take into the following weekend's home game against Irish. For his part, Mallinder was refusing to fret, remaining level-headed in the Allianz Park press room after the game and insisting there was no growing anxiety about the recent run of league defeats.

'We played pretty well at Sale last week and we changed the team a little bit, but we're not playing as well as we were before the Six Nations,' he said. 'We played well during the Six Nations as well and we're not too concerned about the current run.

'We were playing Saracens, who are top of the league, and they're a good side, but we played into their hands a little bit.

'We fell into the hands of Sarries' rush defence and we're disappointed because the accuracy of our game wasn't there today. But the pleasing thing was that we showed character to come back.'

That character would certainly be tested to the maximum in the week that followed, with Saints well aware that they could not afford any more slip-ups.

While there was no panic, there was realism, especially from Wood, who told his team-mates that they must turn their form around quickly if they were to stay in the hunt for silverware.

'We're all professional players and we've got to look to get back on the horse and get back into the Saints way of doing things,' Wood said. 'We pride ourselves on that.

'Whether it's down to the Six Nations players coming back, I don't know, but we haven't quite functioned as well as we should have during the past few weeks. We've got to do it quickly because we're running out of time.'

After testing games against Sale, Leicester and Saracens, there was certainly real confidence that Saints could overcome a London Irish team shorn of key men such as James O'Connor and Topsy Ojo. However, the pressure that had been piled on the team would certainly be a factor and each player was searching for a return to top form. Elliott was one of those men, with the wing stressing his desire to regain his try-scoring spark. He had not scored since the victory against Bath back in December and was licking his lips at facing Irish, who he scored his first hat-trick against in a home game during the previous season.

If Elliott was to get back in business, Saints would need to create chances against Irish and there was a real desire to open up the men from the Madejski Stadium in the bid to provide a big confidence boost after a flat few weeks for the Franklin's Gardens outfit.

Game 33: Sunday, 20 April 2014: Northampton Saints 36 London Irish 21 (Aviva Premiership – round 20)

Saints: Foden (Wilson 62); Elliott, G Pisi, Burrell, North; Myler, Fotuali'i; A Waller (E Waller 55 (A Waller 65)), McMillan, Ma'afu (Denman 55), Manoa (Clark 40 (Williams 63 (McMillan 69))), Lawes, Dowson, Wood (c), Dickinson (van Velze 60 (Ma'afu 69)).

London Irish: Lewington (Homer 45); Yarde, Mulchrone, Sheridan, Fenby; Geraghty (c) (Dorrian 75), O'Leary (Allinson 45); Parr (Harris 70), Mayhew (Hagan 47), Halavatau, Low (Evans 33), Rouse, Cowan (Sinclair 50), Ellis, Treviranus.

Referee: JP Doyle

Attendance: 13,475

Tries: Saints: Jamie Elliott (2), Kahn Fotuali'i, Salesi Ma'afu, Alex Waller. **London Irish:** Andy Fenby, Shane Geraghty, Jebb Sinclair

Conversions: Saints: Stephen Myler (3), James Wilson. **London Irish:** Shane Geraghty (3)

Penalties: Saints: Stephen Myler.

Five tries, five points, job done.

That was the outcome for Saints on Easter Sunday, though how they got there was far from plain sailing.

Instead they were forced to weather a late storm, which could have grown even more severe had Marland Yarde's try stood.

Yarde galloped clear unopposed before dotting down, feeling he'd done enough to bring his team back to just one point behind, presuming the conversion was made.

The Saints fans, players and coaches were jittery enough without that, but, thankfully for everyone of a green, black and gold persuasion, the score was ruled out for a forward pass.

It was a lucky escape and one which Jim Mallinder's men took advantage of to record a 36-21 success.

That it was ever that close came from Irish's ability, which was evident in the early stages as, orchestrated by the enigmatic Shane Geraghty, they played a creative game.

And it also came from Saints dropping their high standards, which had seen them surge into a 29-0 lead when popular Australian prop Salesi Ma'afu drew roars of approval with his first score for the club.

Mallinder pointed out after the game that his team must be better than this should they make the play-offs.

And while that is true, you have to feel the intensity of a knock-out encounter, which should be a lot closer than this, will ensure a similar series of events don't unfold.

This was not the best way to win a game, but it was certainly entertaining stuff, with two teams who wanted to play.

It was reminiscent of the victory over Worcester in September 2012, when Saints led 37-3 before leaving the door open and stumbling over the line at 37-31.

Saints played a similarly open game on this occasion, earning a couple of slick scores, including two for Jamie Elliott, who ended his near-four-month try drought with a double.

And Irish showed an abundance of spark in that spirited fightback.

Overall, though, Brian Smith's men left with nothing.

To Saints went the spoils. And that was all you could ask for.

Because while the desired destination is important, it doesn't really matter how you get there, as long as you do.

Saints are going the right way about it, and have now racked up nine wins from ten home games this season, putting 30-plus points past all but three teams: Newcastle, Harlequins and Leicester.

That is some record, and one they should take confidence from in the final weeks of the season.

There is much to play for and, should they achieve their aims this season, no one will remember what happened in the final 35 minutes against Irish.

If they don't, however, this performance will be looked upon as a precursor for later events. It is up to Saints to make sure it is the former rather than the latter.

Elliott and Saints did manage to end their respective barren runs in this fixture, but, as expected, the nerves were jangling at the conclusion of this clash at the Gardens.

It was far more fraught with danger than had initially appeared the case as Mallinder's men surged into a big lead, with tries galore. There was even one for Ma'afu, who was a hugely popular scorer, earning the biggest roar of the day as he threw himself over the line.

However, Irish, who had taken a real beating at times, with Shane Geraghty being sick on the pitch after one sledgehammer hit from George Pisi, showed bravery to battle back. They really rattled Saints, who eventually regained control of the game and finished things off with an Alex Waller try.

The win pushed Saints seven points clear of Leicester and Bath in the race to finish second – Saracens were plenty of points clear in first – but Mallinder was not exactly delighted with the way his team left the door open for an Irish comeback.

'The first ten minutes of the second half was pretty good, but we got our bonus point and then seemed to slip off,' he said. 'It got a little bit squeaky and it's really disappointing.

'It's a game where we could have finished with a convincing win but it ended up being a little bit in the balance.

'We came back well in the end and with 14 men [after Waller was sin-binned] there was a massive scrum that was key.

'The last ten minutes we got that intensity back, but we need to be better when we come up against the good sides later this season. We need to be better than we were today.

'One of the big positives is that we got the five points and it is in our hands with two games to go. We just need to keep winning and we've got a very good chance of getting that home semi-final.'

Thoughts of the Premiership semi-final would soon be put on the back burner, with focus switching to another final-four tie that would come on the Friday that followed.

Harlequins would be heading to the Gardens, hoping to spoil Saints' chances of setting up an Amlin Challenge Cup Final appearance at Cardiff Arms Park in May.

One big problem ahead of that European tie was to come in the form of an injury crisis that revolved around the role of hooker. Main men Hartley and Haywood were sidelined with shoulder injuries and Matti Williams had sustained a broken leg in the win against Irish.

It left Ross McMillan with a big role to play against Harlequins and the former farmer conducted one of the interviews of the season in the build-up to the big game.

McMillan opened up on how he lost 26kgs during his first pre-season at the club and he talked about his life before arriving at Franklin's Gardens, revealing how he would get up at 5am to help his wife milk cows while working for a family who did beef and sheep farming.

The likeable forward had certainly come a long way since those days and it was heart-warming to hear just how grateful he was for his big chance at Northampton, discussing what it meant to him to have his name on a shirt in the Saints dressing room. That No.2 jersey would be his own against Quins – though Haywood was fit enough to take a place on the bench – and he and the rest of the players were determined to book their place in a second final of the season after having already reached the LV= Cup showpiece.

'We've had the better of results against them this season, but we know Friday's a different entity and we've got to be at our best to get the right result,' said Myler ahead of the game.

Saints had certainly turned the tide against Quins in recent seasons and the confidence they had shown in the early stages of the clash with Irish was transferred into this encounter.

However, while the pressure was the same, the opposition was stronger, with Quins starting to gain momentum and the likes of Mike Brown and Danny Care being named in the team for the game at the Gardens, making the Challenge Cup semi-final an extremely difficult proposition.

Mallinder rested Foden and put Lawes, Wood and Burrell among a strong set of replacements, but there were just four changes overall and the desire to book the ticket to the Welsh capital was clear as the focus sharpened on another knock-out clash.

Game 34: Friday, 25 April 2014: Northampton Saints 18 Harlequins 10 (Amlin Challenge Cup semi-final)

Saints: Wilson; Elliott, G Pisi, Stephenson (Burrell 67), North (Collins 21); Myler, Fotuali'i (Glynn 78); A Waller (Denman 72), McMillan (Haywood 67), Ma'afu (Mercey 53), Manoa (Lawes 58), Craig, Clark (Wood 58), Dowson (c), Dickinson.

Harlequins: Brown (Lindsay-Hague 40); Walker, Molenaar, Turner-Hall (Grimoldby 71), Smith; Botica, Care (K Dickson 59); Marler (Lambert 59), Ward, Sinckler (Doran-Jones 71), Matthews, Robson (Guest 34), Wallace (Fa'asavalu 45), Robshaw (c), Easter.

Referee: George Clancy

Attendance: 10,077

Tries: Saints: Tom Collins, Kahn Fotuali'i. **Harlequins:** Nick Easter

Conversions: Saints: Stephen Myler. **Harlequins:** Ben Botica

Penalties: Saints: Stephen Myler (2). **Harlequins:** Ben Botica

---

There was a frisson of excitement around Franklin's Gardens on Friday night as Saints' swagger returned.

It hadn't been seen since mid-March, but Jim Mallinder's men finally rediscovered their best form at the expense of Harlequins.

There was tempo to their play, aggression and a dogged determination in defence that left Quins, with their quartet of England stars, reeling.

Danny Care, Mike Brown, who went off injured at half-time, Joe Marler and Chris Robshaw were powerless to prevent their side slipping to an 18-10 defeat.

Instead it was Saints' squad which came to the fore, with none of the men who represented England in the Six Nations Championship in the starting line-up.

It was reminiscent of the times during that tournament when players came from nowhere, stepped up to the plate and drove the club forward.

It gave the England players another reminder of the talent that is lying in wait if they fail to perform, and that can only be a good thing ahead of a huge few weeks.

Saints now have an Amlin Challenge Cup Final to look forward to, added to an Aviva Premiership play-off semi-final. And the European progression is undoubtedly a good thing as it eases a little pressure in the pursuit of silverware. Should Saints win the Amlin, it could prove to be the catalyst for Premiership success. Why? Because the club go into the game at Cardiff on 23 May having lost their past four finals.

If they were to win the European encounter, it could inject the belief needed to secure the league title, presuming Saints make it through the semi-final tie.

With the kind of form they showed at the Gardens on Friday night, Mallinder's men are capable of achieving their aims.

They now need to ensure they remain on an upward curve going into a month that could become the best in the club's history.

It may be the Susan Boyle to the Heineken Cup's Beyonce, but the Amlin Challenge Cup was providing plenty of reasons for Saints supporters to sing.

The convincing quarter-final win at Sale Sharks was so precious during a tough time and this success against Harlequins not only set up a shot at glory in Cardiff on May 23, but it helped Saints to maintain the momentum garnered in the victory against London Irish.

Fotuali'i showed his class, with the Samoan star pulling the strings superbly throughout. He scored one try and set up the other for Collins as Saints charged into an 18-3 lead before Quins, who had posed little threat, replied with a try in the second half.

'Kahn's a special player,' said Mallinder after the game. 'There were two outstanding nines on the field and Danny Care, as we've seen over the last few weeks, has been in great form. I think we marshalled him well and I thought Kahn was outstanding. He's a quality player and we've got Lee Dickson as well, who has got a little bit of a knock as well, so we're very, very lucky we've got some quality scrum halves at the club.'

Not only had Saints got the job done, but they had also managed to keep some key men on ice for the following week's clash with Bath at the Recreation Ground. It was a win-win for Mallinder, whose only worry came in the form of North, who had been forced off with a calf strain.

For the fans, the biggest anxiety during the days that followed came from the lack of tickets that were to be allocated for the Challenge Cup Final. Saints had only been given a 1,000-ticket allocation and they were to sell out in the space of just 24 hours.

It was clear that European glory meant a lot to everyone at the club, but winning a first Premiership title was still top of the agenda, and the game at Bath was looming large on the horizon.

Saints were closing in on securing that prized top-two spot and they knew that a win in the West Country could make it certain. They would have to do without North, who was to miss out, and moves were made to solve another injury problem.

The lack of options at hooker was still causing a headache for Mallinder, with Hartley and Williams still unavailable, and former Gloucester man Koree Britton was brought in. He would be a travelling reserve at the Recreation Ground, where Saints would be in for a tough time against a Bath team who had play-off aspirations of their own.

In fact, there was a school of thought that Mallinder's men would have been better off losing at fourth-placed Bath because it could help Saints avoid third-placed Leicester in the play-offs.

After all, if you were to pick a fight with a big bloke, you'd rather take on the one you'd knocked down in your past five meetings than the one who had his foot on your throat for the previous ten.

However, thoughts of recent struggles against Tigers were for another day and all Saints could worry about as they made the trip to the West Country was getting the job done and making sure their play-off semi-final would be played at home.

Mallinder opted to field his strongest possible side in the bid to put it to bed once and for all and to ensure there would be no final-day wobbles when Wasps came to the Gardens.

However, full strength or not, Saints still knew they had a huge task on their hands to win at the home of a Bath team who had won 26 of their 33 games during the campaign and who had plenty of players capable of causing problems.

It was set up to be a cracker, but West warned his forwards of the size of the task that awaited them, while Burrell insisted that playing pretty rugby wouldn't be the way to beat Bath. Saints knew they were in for a real scrap, but after back-to-back wins, the belief was coursing through the veins again and there was a palpable feeling that they could get the win that would provide crucial wriggle room against Wasps eight days later.

Game 35: Friday, 2 May 2014: Bath 19 Northampton Saints 19 (Aviva Premiership – round 21)

Bath: Abendanon; Watson (Agulla 73), Joseph, Devoto (Henson 71), Banahan; Ford, Young (Stringer 63); James, Webber (Batty 18 (Catt 55)), Wilson (Perenise 55), Hooper (c), Attwood (Day 71), Fearns, Mercer, Houston.

Saints: Foden; K Pisi, G Pisi, Burrell, Elliott; Myler, Fotuali'i; A Waller (Denman 71), McMillan (Haywood 55), Ma'afu (Mercey 55), Manoa (Craig 55), Lawes, Clark (Dowson 55), Wood (c), Dickinson.

Referee: Matthew Carley

Attendance: 11,978

Tries: Bath: George Ford. **Saints:** Jamie Elliott

Conversions: Bath: George Ford. **Saints:** Stephen Myler

Penalties: Bath: George Ford (4). **Saints:** Stephen Myler (4)

Draws are so rare in rugby that when they do occur teams can sometimes be slightly unsure what to make of them.

Saints have sampled two stalemates this season, but there can be no doubt that Friday night's 19-19 draw at Bath felt very different to the one at Leicester back in October.

At Welford Road, Jim Mallinder's men surrendered a ten-point lead and were clinging on at the end as they stumbled over the line to earn their two points.

But at Bath, relief rather than regret was the overriding emotion, with a controversial ending crowning a topsy-turvy encounter. At half-time, Saints would not have settled for the 6-6 scoreline with which they headed into the dressing room to regroup. They had bossed the first period, with attack after attack bouncing back off the defiant blue and white wall.

Bath had used the little territory they had to good effect, earning enough shots at goal to ensure they wouldn't be behind at the interval.

And by the time referee Matthew Carley blew the final whistle amid a backdrop of boos from the home fans, Saints were more than happy to share the spoils.

Because Bath had upped the tempo after the break, with George Ford the fulcrum of their attacking game.

Saints showed great character to stick with their hosts, who were building up a head of steam after Ford's majestic try.

And, thankfully for Northampton, they had an equally impressive fly half in their camp, with Stephen Myler again showing why he is known as the Iceman by his team-mates.

Myler kept his cool to land a tricky conversion and a late penalty, among others, as well as teeing up Jamie Elliott for a try with a sublime offload.

It was a tale of two fly halves. A story written by two of England's best 10s.

But the sub-plot was that Saints had done what they needed to do, and that was shown by the smile adorning Mallinder's face during post-match media duties.

He knew his team had pretty much secured their top-two place, with next week's game against Wasps able to be used as a warm-up act for the main event of the play-offs a week later.

That is what Saints wanted, and that is why the Recreation Ground draw tasted sweet as opposed to sour.

If the win against Harlequins owed much to Fotuali'i, Saints salvaging a draw from their trip to the Recreation Ground was very much about his half-back partner. Myler was simply superb as he ensured his side would share the spoils and all but secure the home semi-final they wanted.

The fly half matched rival George Ford stride for stride, with his back door pass to Elliott for Saints' only try of the game simply superb and his pressure kicking again so accurate.

He had again landed a late penalty that earned vital points and Myler was becoming more and more important to his team's chances of success. In fact, it had got to the point where there was a real worry about just what would happen without him.

The consequences of his absence had been shown during Saints' sticky run a month earlier, and they knew they simply could not afford to lose him for any part of May.

Instead, they would need their Iceman to help keep them cool as the race for two pieces of silverware continued to hot up, and Mallinder knew just how vital the man he had invested his faith in at No.10 now was to the team's chances of glory.

'Stephen is really good under pressure,' Mallinder said. 'That conversion from the touchline was important, as well as the penalty right at the death.

'He stood up under a lot of pressure and I'm pleased for him and the team.'

Myler was happy to conduct post-match interview duties after the game, but, typically, he played down his own role in the draw, despite the fact he had a hand in all 19 of his side's points.

That kind of steady character mixed with the immense accuracy in his game was admirable and it was going to be a big month for the man who had made the fly half role his own during a stellar season.

Saints could also look forward to surrounding him with more stars, with North, Corbisiero, Hartley, Christian Day and Lee Dickson also closing in on a return after missing the Bath draw.

Mallinder's men looked in fine fettle for the most important part of the season, with momentum building and the cavalry coming back to boost the charge towards an historic double.

However, no one was getting too carried away, with the final-day clash with Wasps lying in wait at the Gardens. Saints needed just a single point from that game to make sure of a top-two spot, and they were on an almost inevitable collision course with their local rivals.

Leicester Tigers boss Cockerill got a dig in early as he insisted his team would rather face Saints than Saracens in the play-off semi-finals and that would only add further fuel to the Northampton fire.

'It is only down the road and we have got a pretty good record against them,' Cockerill had said.

'Saracens have played very well this season and the plastic pitch is not perfect for us. We are old school at Leicester, we like grass and mud.

'Wherever you go in a one-off game, it is massive and there will be lots of pressure for both sides. We will take our chances.'

First, Saints needed to take their own chances against Wasps, with the players insisting that only a top-two finish would be good enough now they had put themselves in such a commanding position.

The bid to cement that home tie was strengthened by the return of North, who had recovered from his calf injury, as well as Christian Day and Lee Dickson, who were also back in the starting 15.

There was great news on the bench, as Corbisiero got set to make his first club appearance since October, while Britton also looked set to get some game time as the new hooker was named among a strong set of replacements.

Wasps were not quite taking the clash as seriously as they rested the likes of James Haskell, Joe Simpson and Matt Mullan ahead of their crucial Champions Cup play-off against Stade Francais, with the winner of the two-leg affair getting entry into Europe's top tier competition the following season.

The fact the away side were leaving men out left the door wide open for Saints to get the big win they wanted as they sought to storm into the semi-final on the following Friday night. For Mallinder's men it was all about emerging victorious, ensuring key men did not sustain any injuries and maintaining their momentum ahead of what looked likely to be another meeting with their enemy from up the M1.

Defeat would most likely bring a trip to Welford Road in the play-offs, and with Saints having not won on Leicester territory since 2007, they knew there simply could not be any slip-ups against a weakened Wasps team.

Game 36: Saturday, 10 May 2014: Northampton Saints 74 Wasps 13 (Aviva Premiership – round 22)

Saints: Foden; K Pisi, Wilson, Burrell (Stephenson 46), North; Myler (G Pisi 53), L Dickson (Fotuali'i 70); A Waller (Corbisiero 53), Haywood (Britton 60), Ma'afu (Mercey 40), Craig, C Day (Manoa 76), Clark, Dowson (c), Dickinson (Wood 70).

Wasps: T Bell (Goode 56); Short, C Bell (c), Hayter (Daly 65), Varndell; Carlisle, Davies (Sheehan 59); McIntyre (Reeves 59), Lindsay (Festuccia 67), Vea (Swainston 55), Cannon (Launchbury 65), Palmer, Jackson (Johnson 68), Thompson, Hughes.

Referee: Luke Pearce

Attendance: 13,459

Tries: Saints: George North (2), Phil Dowson (2), Stephen Myler, Luther Burrell, Ben Foden, Lee Dickson (2), Ken Pisi, Tom Stephenson. **Wasps:** Charlie Davies, Tom Varndell

Conversions: Saints: Stephen Myler (3), James Wilson (5)

Penalties: Saints: Stephen Myler. **Wasps:** Joe Carlisle

Well, that escalated quickly ...

Saints seemed in a slumber after falling 13 points behind inside the first 15 minutes, but what happened next was simply stunning.

Eleven tries and a total of 74 points amassed in a victory that was the eighth biggest in Premiership history, and the largest since February 2005.

Wasps wilted in the heat of the Franklin's Gardens inferno and Jim Mallinder's men had the perfect boost ahead of the serious matters that beckon in the next couple of weeks.

Make no mistake, what happened on Saturday could be so important in the context of this season.

If Saints can harness the confidence and belief garnered from this performance, they will be tough to stop in the pursuit of silverware.

But, if they allow themselves to get carried away – something that boss Mallinder refused to do after the game – it could come back to bite them.

Mallinder was, typically, cool as a cucumber in his post-match press conference, allowing himself a smile and a joke with the media, but stressing the hard work starts now.

And he's right. No offence to Wasps, but you could have written their defensive tactics on the back of a cigarette packet.

They were all at sea from the moment George North danced his way through their porous rearguard, leaving two men in amber chewing on the Gardens grass. It was a procession from that point, with each try greeted with an increased roar from the home fans.

They enjoyed this – and why not? It was a continuation of some sensational performances on home turf this season.

But, while they have racked up a humongous 391 points in 11 home Premiership games (an average of 35 points per outing), Saints know there is one team they have not beaten at the Gardens this season: Leicester.

Tigers loom large on the horizon this week and Northampton will need every ounce of self-assurance if they are to end their winless run against their rivals.

There will be constant reminders of the fact Saints have not secured a victory against the Tigers since September 2010 in the build-up to the latest East Midlands instalment.

But Mallinder's men should not look any further back than the Saturday when they put 74 points past Wasps.

They should store that feel-good vibe and take it into the Tigers clash.

They have worked so hard to get a home semi-final in the month of May – their first play-off match at the Gardens since 2010. Now they must make it pay.

There were times during this match that it almost felt cruel. Saints overcame their sloppy start and swarmed all over Wasps, relentlessly putting them to the sword and emerging with their biggest victory of the season.

A total of 11 tries were scored by Mallinder's men as they cruised to victory and got the perfect boost ahead of what was confirmed as a home play-off semi-final against Leicester on the following Friday.

However, Wasps director of rugby Dai Young was not overly impressed with his side's convincing conquerors, instead raising doubts about their ability to alter plans when needed. 'The big difference between teams like Leicester coming here to ourselves is that they can handle the forward power and that would force Northampton into plan B,' Young said. 'We know how effective plan A is, but have they got enough outside of that? I feel Leicester will match them in that area.

'Northampton have added a lot this season, with George North and the likes, so they should be a more rounded team this season. I certainly wouldn't like to call it.

'I'm sure Leicester feel they can come here and do the job, but it's going to be really tough.'

Mallinder pointed out just how difficult he felt that Tigers fixture would be, but he was far from fazed as he reflected on the Wasps win and, inevitably, looked ahead to the biggest game of the season.

'This win gives us confidence, but we won't read too much into it,' said Mallinder, who had been boosted by the return from injury of Corbisiero during the second half. 'Wasps sent a weakened side with their minds on next week, and we're not daft enough to think otherwise.

'What we take out of it is that we've won and we've got our home semi-final. After 22 games, that's all you can ask for. We've got it and we know we're in good shape.

'We've got a good squad, good options and selection is going to be tricky this week to make sure we get our best starting 15.

'We're physically and mentally in good shape but we know it's going to be difficult against Leicester. They will come down here very confident, but we're looking forward to it.'

Everyone was looking forward to it. From the coaches, to the players, to the fans.

There was going to be a buzz around the Gardens throughout the week that followed and it was all about how Saints handled that and the expectation that a home East

Midlands derby would bring. However, you always got the feeling they would relish it.

That they had a point to prove against a team they had not beaten since September 2010. That Cockerill could just be eating his words about preferring to play Saints rather than Saracens.

Cockerill, who had seen his side beat Saracens 31-27 in their final game of the regular season, at Welford Road, was to continue using the media to play some traditional pre-match mind games as he insisted the pressure was all on Saints.

'It's a local derby in a semi-final and all the pressure is on them – not us,' Cockerill said. 'They have had the season of their lives – now they have got to finish it off.

'But we know we are a good side on our day and we have done all right against them in the past few years.

'That was some turnaround from them against Wasps, being 13-0 down and going on to win 74-13. Fair play to them. They are a good side.

'If they get momentum, they will punish you. We rested the core of our team against Saracens whereas Saints played most of theirs.'

Mallinder didn't want to waste too much of his pre-match press conference discussing Cockerill's comments. Instead he just labelled them 'rubbish' and attempted to get on with talking about his own team.

'We don't read any of that,' Mallinder said. 'It's rubbish.

'We're just concentrating on getting our own house in order, that's the main thing.

'You only listen to what you want to listen to and read what you want to read. We don't get involved in that at all. We don't talk about it, don't even read it to be honest. It's rubbish.'

Things were certainly getting spicy with the fire stoked ahead of a game that needed no added fireworks. One big question that loomed large was about who would referee the East Midlands bout. Would it be Barnes again? Or would someone else get the gig?

Four days before the game, it was confirmed that Barnes would not be involved, with JP Doyle, who had refereed Saints' draw at Welford Road earlier in the season, handed the role as man in the middle.

That took a little of the sting out of things and rather than discussing referees, Saints could simply focus on what they had to do to finally end their horror run against their rivals.

Leicester had held the bragging rights for too long and Saints were desperate to overcome them to book a spot in the Premiership Final for the second season in succession.

A familiar voice had a few words for his old team, with Soane Tonga'uiha, who had played in the showpiece against Leicester in 2013, taking a call in France and stressing he felt his old club could get the win they wanted.

As for the current crop of players, Ken Pisi was also vocalising his belief in the squad, insisting this was his team's time to finally topple the Tigers.

'They've got that upper hand psychologically, but we've been getting closer and closer and I believe that Friday will be our time to get a win,' Pisi said.

'We've definitely got the belief. We're confident, whoever's playing, and even our bench is strong. We've got a good vibe all round.'

The clock was ticking down and the time for talking was almost over. All that was left for Mallinder to do was to set his team selection in stone and hope that the men he picked could perform his orders on the pitch.

Several big guns were to return to the starting 15, with George Pisi, Fotuali'i, Wood and Manoa all in the team after being used as replacements in the win against Wasps. Lawes was also back, but Hartley remained sidelined with his shoulder problem. Dowson was captain in his absence.

Tigers, who were on the brink of a tenth successive Premiership Final, also brought back the likes of Tom Youngs and Logovi'i Mulipola after resting them against Saracens and it was shaping up to be one of the most ferocious collisions in Premiership history.

Mallinder called on the Saints supporters to do their bit, urging them to roar their team to Twickenham. Those words were certainly heeded and the atmosphere was electric ahead of kick-off.

Some fans took their place on the Gordon Terrace almost two hours before the game began, with noise filtering around the ground like never before. It was an incredible build-up to what promised to be an incredible game, and you could just sense that this was different.

You could feel how much this meant to the fans that continued to flock into the ground to join the hardy bunch on the terrace and the fact that it was a Friday night brought an extra spark to proceedings.

Ten long matches had gone by without Saints slaying Tigers, and supporters were so desperate for their team to finally present them with a chance to lord it over their Leicester counterparts.

However, this was about more than just going into work happy on a Monday, it was about booking that trip to Twickenham. It was about crowning a memorable season with the club's first Premiership triumph. It was about banishing all those years of near misses.

It was Saints against Leicester and it was going to be a noisy meeting between neighbours. Nerves were jangling, in the stands and in the dressing room, but everyone was united by a common aim: to win an East Midlands derby and set up a shot at Grand Final glory.

Game 37: Friday, 16 May 2014: Northampton Saints 21 Leicester Tigers 20 (Aviva Premiership play-off semi-final)

Saints: Foden; Collins (Mercey 55), G Pisi (Wilson 66), Burrell, North; Myler, Fotuali'i (Dickson 62); A Waller (Corbisiero 51), Haywood, Ma'afu, Manoa (Day 69), Lawes, Dowson (c) (Clark 55), Wood, Dickinson.

Leicester: Tait (Mafi 61); Morris, Tuilagi, Bowden, Goneva; Flood (Williams 62), B Youngs; Ayerza, T Youngs, Mulipola, Deacon (Kitchener 68), Slater (c), Gibson (Briggs 57 (Thompstone 68)), Salvi, Crane.

Referee: JP Doyle

Attendance: 13,491

Tries: Saints: George North, Tom Wood. **Leicester Tigers:** Manu Tuilagi, Ben Youngs

Conversions: Saints: Stephen Myler. **Leicester Tigers:** Toby Flood (2)

Penalties: Saints: Stephen Myler (3). **Leicester Tigers:** Toby Flood, Owen Williams

This was a moment in time. A moment when you looked around and all you saw was elation.

A moment Saints fans had waited almost four years for. A moment when every one of them didn't care whether they saw another rugby game again, because they had seen this one.

This was a moment when ten games' worth of hurt washed away.

A moment when all that was said in the build-up to this fractious East Midlands derby, and all the other East Midlands derbies, mattered not.

This was a moment to tell the grandchildren about. It was an eternal moment.

Why did this moment matter so much?

This moment mattered because there have been no moments like this since September 2010.

There have been other moments. There has been Dublin. There has been Belfast. There was Allianz Park. But those moments were nothing compared to this.

This was a moment that lasted a second, but felt like it lasted a lifetime.

What was this moment? This moment was Stephen Myler kicking the ball out to end the match. To set up another chance of glory in two weeks' time.

Twickenham beckons for a second season in succession. And this time, Leicester will not be there.

Leicester will not be there for the first time in ten seasons.

At that, you have to take a pause. Should the men in white coats be called for? Should you be carted away for thinking Tigers have not made the Grand Final?

Did Saints really just beat a Leicester side whose defence was immense for so long? A Leicester side who had a man advantage for the closing stages of this game?

They did.

Was controversial official Wayne Barnes not there to ride in and wreck the fairytale story?

He was not.

This time, the man charging in was Tom Wood. All that was lacking was the white horse.

And is there a more deserving Saints hero?

There is not.

Wood, a man who has seen so many bad moments and fronted up to every single one of them, had earned this.

He had earned it for facing the media after last year's savage Premiership Final, taking up the captain's role from the red-carded Dylan Hartley. He had earned it for facing the media after the 40-7 home humbling against Leinster back

190

in December. He had earned it for the lack of a win against Leicester since his Saints debut against the very same side.

But he wasn't the only one who merited this. Every single person in green, black and gold warranted what happened at the denouement of this game.

The Saints fans definitely deserved this. The noise levels were deafening towards the end. The Burrda Stand sucked two tries in.

This atmosphere was like nothing heard before in this part of Northampton.

The Gardens was rocking. And why?

Because this moment meant so much. And this moment was what everyone of a Saints persuasion had dreamed off during the entirety of their working week. They would have paid double, treble, quadruple the ticket price to see this moment. Now they want to see a moment even more special than this one. They want to see a moment that involves a big trophy lifted in the air.

At Cardiff on Friday night, they want to see that moment.

But the moment that would mean most could come at Twickenham eight days later. And that moment is still in sight thanks to an unforgettable Friday night at Franklin's Gardens.

When Myler booted the ball out of play to bring this historic East Midlands encounter to its epic conclusion, a black cloud was removed from the skies above Franklin's Gardens.

Saints had finally beaten their old rivals and a wave of emotion swept the stands and the field of play.

On the pitch, players in green, black and gold hugged each other and punched the air, while those of a Tigers persuasion slumped, disconsolate, on the turf.

In the stands, there was pandemonium as supporters frantically gasped for air, trying to take in what they had just witnessed.

In the press box, professionalism went out of the window, with those from Northampton unashamedly smiling from ear to ear at an event that meant so much to the people of the town.

Among the Saints coaches, there were gleeful embraces and unbridled celebrations, with boss Mallinder the most animated of the lot, clenching his fists tightly and grinning as he received the congratulations of King and West.

Tigers director of rugby Cockerill stood, still, sucking on his teeth as he gave off the look of a man who had just swallowed a wasp and was desperately searching for a way to relieve himself of the pain it was causing him.

That reaction was understandable because Saints had snatched victory from the jaws of defeat.

Ma'afu had been sent off for landing two punches on Tigers hooker Tom Youngs and it looked like yet another derby would end in disaster for Saints, who were forced to battle back from 17-6 down with just 14 men.

North and, two minutes from time, Wood went over to ensure Mallinder's men seized their chance in the most dramatic fashion, sparking those wild scenes of celebration.

At the conclusion of the game, PA announcer Geoff Allen bellowed out details about tickets for the final at Twickenham, but that was too much to take in and thoughts about heading south would be saved for another day.

At this point, Saints fans were still trying to get their heads around what had happened and what it meant for the club. It was the same for the players and coaches, who were quickly thrust into the media spotlight.

Mallinder and Wood were the men charged with answering questions from the Northampton perspective and both did well to be as calm as they were.

'It was a very good game of rugby,' said Mallinder, further enhancing his status as the master of understatement.

'A lot of credit to Leicester. They've come here, they're a good team, they've been to ten successive finals and it's a credit to them.

'Both sides put in good performances, but I think we just deserved it in the end.

'We went in at half-time down, but we said we had to keep playing and moving their front five around.

'To go down to 14 men for the last ten minutes or so and still get that try was a massive testament to the character of the squad.'

However, did Mallinder really think his team could come back from such a deficit after Ma'afu was sent off in the 56th minute?

'We thought we could,' he said.

'We didn't want to get into an arm wrestle against Leicester – they're good at that. They want to slow things down and we wanted to keep the tempo high. Kahn [Fotuali'i] started that and Lee Dickson and the rest of the subs kept that going.'

Wood emerged from the Saints dressing room to conduct his interview and it was a typically considered one, despite the drama that preceded it.

'It's a pretty big win,' he said. 'You saw what it meant to the fans. The atmosphere was a couple of levels up to what I've felt at the Gardens.

'It's about us giving them something to cheer about and that just snowballs. In the last ten minutes, it's them that keeps us going and pushes us around the field.

'It's really significant in the town and it's significant to us. We've always known we've had it in us, but, for some reason, on big days we've stalled.

'We've given ourselves a mountain to climb in the past and failed to finish the job. It's hugely frustrating to know you've got it in the tank and not deliver on the big days.

'I'm just so glad we stuck it out and got the result.'

However, while the nature of the victory made it feel like Saints had actually won the league that night, they hadn't. In fact, they hadn't won anything during what was turning out to be one of the most memorable seasons in the club's history.

A day after the win against Tigers, their Premiership Final opponents were confirmed, with familiar foes Saracens the side that would await them in the Twickenham showpiece.

The next two weeks would decide whether the name of Northampton would be etched on one trophy, two trophies or no trophies at all, and the huge challenge for Saints was to make sure that the Challenge Cup Final did not feel like it was after the Lord Mayor's show.

Mallinder had to motivate his men again, making sure they continued on an upward curve for two more gargantuan games that would ultimately decide whether the season was one of success, or another of eventual failure.

'A significant moment will be when we win the final of a big competition,' said Mallinder, rallying his troops as he tried to put that glorious win against the old rival to bed as quickly as possible.

'We were in the final of the Heineken Cup [in 2011], we were in the final of the Premiership last season, so a significant moment will be when we win a big one.

'We've got two finals in two weeks to look forward to.

'We've already been in an LV= Cup Final and didn't manage to win that one, but we've got two chances to bring some silverware back to the people of Northampton.'

Mallinder would have the Ma'afu situation to deal with in the week leading up to the Bath game as the Australian prop faced a disciplinary hearing.

Having seen him in the car park at the awards do on the eve of that hearing, it was clear that he was far from confident about his chances of pulling on a Saints shirt again during the season, with the player expecting to be banned for at least two weeks.

However, Ma'afu was to get something of a reprieve, picking up just a one-week suspension that would see him miss the Challenge Cup Final but be available to square up to Saracens in the battle for the league title. It was a big boost for Saints, who had been keen to keep their scrum settled, and it was another reason to feel like this could be the year things went the club's way in the desperate search for silverware.

At the awards evening, Manoa was named Saints' supporters' player of the year for the second season in succession, crowning yet another fine campaign for the big American.

Day picked up the players' player of the year award, with a nice video accompanying his prize as his team-mates paid tribute to a man they labelled a 'line-out nause'. Ethan Waller was also a winner as he received the young player of the year prize.

However, the players would not be staying long that night as they exited early to prepare for the big game against Bath in Cardiff a few days later.

In truth, everyone's thoughts were on that match and the one that would follow, meaning celebrating the season was kept on ice for a couple more weeks.

'It's a really difficult balance because there's a huge amount to celebrate from Friday and everyone's positive but, feet on the ground, we want to finish the job,' Wood said.

'We don't want that to be the end of the season. We want some silverware to take away.

'It's about regrouping and recovery because it was a brutal encounter. We won't be knocking seven bells out of each other, it's all about getting the mind right for another big clash.

'Bath are a quality team and Saracens won't be easy, either!'

Mallinder had hinted that he would make changes for the Challenge Cup Final, but he decided against making too many, instead switching just five as he looked to get the balance right before the big one against Saracens.

Mercey came in at tighthead for Ma'afu, while Dickson replaced Fotuali'i at scrum half and Clark was in for Dowson. Ken Pisi returned from injury and came in for Collins, who had performed so admirably after being thrown in at late notice against Tigers, while Corbisiero was a starter, taking the place of Alex Waller.

Bath were boosted by the presence of influential flanker Francois Louw in their starting line-up, but Saints were only focusing on themselves, feeling this was a chance to set themselves up for a special finish to the season.

Myler, who had kicked all five penalties as Saints beat Bourgoin 15-3 to win the Challenge Cup in the 2008/09 season, was urging everyone at the club to make sure that they didn't waste their big chance of a memorable double and he felt victory against Bath would be the catalyst for a first Premiership title.

It was now all about nerve, and North came up with the best way of putting it as he faced the media ahead of a game in his homeland that could bring his first piece of silverware at Saints.

'These are the days that you dig in for in the dark months of December, when you stand on the pitch and can't feel your hands,' the Wales wing said.

'Anyone who plays at this level, if they can't get excited for these days they shouldn't be playing rugby.

'I came to be part of a winning squad. I came to be part of winning silverware. Hopefully I've done enough to be involved in these two finals. It's up to the boss man what he wants to do.

'These are the games you want to play in. You've got to step up and put your big boy pants on.'

Big boy pants on, the Saints players headed across the border in the bid to remove another monkey from their back. They had finally crushed that ten-game Tigers hoodoo, but now they needed to shake off the bridesmaids' tag to win their first final since March 2010.

Game 38: Friday, 23 May 2014: Bath 16 Northampton Saints 30 (Amlin Challenge Cup Final)

Bath: Abendanon; Rokoduguni, Joseph, Devoto (Henson 65), Watson; Ford, Young (Stringer 63); James (Catt 56), Dunn (Guinazu 60), Wilson (Perenise 56), Hooper (c) (Day 72), Attwood, Fearns, Louw, Houston (Mercer 54).

Saints: Foden; K Pisi, G Pisi (Wilson 80), Burrell (Stephenson 77), North; Myler, L Dickson (Fotuali'i 56); Corbisiero (Waller 59), Haywood (McMillan 74), Mercey (Denman 59), Manoa (C Day 65), Lawes, Clark (Dowson 59), Wood (c), Dickinson.

Referee: Jerome Garces (France)

Attendance: 12,843

Tries: Bath: Anthony Watson. **Saints:** Phil Dowson, Ben Foden

Conversions: Bath: George Ford. **Saints:** Stephen Myler

Penalties: Bath: George Ford (3). **Saints:** Stephen Myler (6)

The assembled media were happy with their lot when Tom Wood suddenly extended the post-Amlin Challenge Cup Final press conference with an urge to make a point.

'Could I just say, I'd like to credit the wider squad with tonight's effort,' said Wood. 'Guys have played in the quarter-finals and semi-finals of this competition, people like Ben Nutley, James Craig, Ethan Waller ... too many names to mention.

'It's not just about the 15 or 23 in this game, it's about the whole squad, hence why we got them on the pitch at the end.

'I'm really proud of the depth of our squad, the guys who have stepped up and those who have taken selection on the chin and missed out. I'd like to credit them for it.'

It was yet another measure of Wood's class as a captain as he ensured everyone who had played their part in the Amlin Challenge Cup triumph was given recognition.

And he was right to do so because Saints' European triumph wasn't just forged in Cardiff on Friday night.

It was created with Dublin defiance, Swansea strength, Salford skill and plenty of other ingredients along the way.

Just as reaching the LV= Cup Final had been a sizeable squad effort, this was too.

And at the denouement of this European campaign, that depth told as Bath were blown away in a second half that will have left them shell-shocked.

Things looked to be going so well for the men in blue and white, but when things began to go wrong, they couldn't turn the tide.

This is where Saints have grown as a team during the past few years.

They now know how to pull games out of the fire.

Just as they did against Leicester a week earlier, they retained belief and upped the tempo, leaving the opposition in their slipstream.

Stephen Myler once again played a mammoth role in a recovery, this time from 13-6 down at the break.

He may not get the plaudits George Ford receives, but he once again showed he is the man for the crucial moments.

He landed seven of his eight kicks, missing just once – a late conversion when the game was already won – to help his team over the line.

It was the story of his season and even drew praise from the Bath faithful with one inebriated member of the crowd telling his mate there was no chance, in slightly more colourful language, that Myler would miss before the fly half slotted his sixth penalty of the game.

Myler's 20 points helped Saints secure the silverware, but so did the forward pack's immense power in this final.

So did Kahn Fotuali'i's super-show in the semi-final success against Harlequins, which included a fine score from Tom Collins.

So did Ben Nutley's two-try heroics and Ethan Waller's enormous display on a soggy night at Sale back in April.

So did George Pisi's impressive score against Castres at Franklin's Gardens.

So did George North's brilliant burst against Ospreys at the Liberty Stadium.

So did Jamie Elliott's breakaway score following the most gargantuan of defensive performances at the Aviva Stadium.

So you see, the credits list for this particular success story is as long as Courtney Lawes' legs.

Wood was right: this was about everyone.

And how everyone enjoyed it when that trophy was hoisted high into the Cardiff sky.

Now it's time for the ultimate squad effort – the Premiership season – to end in a similarly happy fashion for this special Saints group.

A trip to the Welsh capital had ended in heartache three years earlier as Leinster destroyed Saints' chances of a European trophy, but the Cardiff curse was finally broken as Mallinder's men ticked off the first of their two massive late-season targets.

Whether it came from the confidence they gained from that titanic tussle with Tigers or the agony of previous final disappointments driving them on, Saints simply refused to be beaten by Bath, sticking dagger after dagger into the men in blue and white after the break.

The West Country outfit had the upper hand before half-time as Ford pulled the strings for them, but he went to pieces during the second period as metronomic Myler once again stepped up for Saints, showing why he had been the top No.10 in England during the campaign.

He displayed his trademark unerring accuracy from the tee, slotting six penalties and a conversion, missing just once as his team turned up the heat during the second period to secure their first trophy in more than four years.

Bath had been 13-6 up heading into the dressing room at the interval, but they could only register three more points as the Saints forwards snarled and Myler's boot brought the trophy to Northampton.

'Stephen was top-drawer,' Mallinder said. 'You need a performance like that in big games. You need someone who can keep their head, make good decisions and not just kick the goals, but I thought our game plan generally was very, very good.

'There's always one or two bits in terms of not getting involved in an arm wrestle and playing some rugby and that's down to the half-backs, who are making those decisions.

'All of our leaders really stepped up.'

They certainly did, and in the press conference that followed, Myler and Wood sat side by side as they looked back over another hugely resilient display.

The flanker paid tribute to the fly half, too, and rightly so, because you felt that while Saints' forwards were buoyed by Myler's refusal to miss, Bath's big men were rattled by Ford's failures from the tee.

That was understandable as if you put in the hard yards, sticking your head in ruck after ruck, you want something to show for it. Saints had points and a trophy, Bath had nothing but cuts and bruises.

However, once again, the celebrations would be kept to a minimum. Yes, players passed through the mixed zone with bottles of beer brought from the dressing room, but there was no wild elation, just a steely determination to sample such joy on a grander scale eight days later.

The players and coaches had come together to spray the Champagne on the Cardiff Arms Park pitch and Wood and Dowson lifted the trophy, but it was just an appetiser for what could happen in the Premiership Final.

Winning the Challenge Cup was a good achievement, but it wasn't the one Saints really wanted. They wanted that first league title and while they would enjoy European success for the weekend, come Monday morning, sights would be set on the trip to the capital.

Saints had unfinished business at English rugby HQ after their defeat to Leicester a year earlier and the man who had been sent off in that game would be back to hand Mallinder a selection dilemma ahead of the showdown with Saracens.

Hartley had watched the Challenge Cup Final from the stands, but his fractured shoulder blade had healed and he was able to be named in the squad for the first time since March.

He would eventually have to make do with a role among the replacements, with Haywood retaining his place at hooker, as Mallinder made some difficult decisions in terms of selection.

The build-up to the final intensified throughout that last week of the season, but there was a feeling that Saints were going into the showpiece in better shape, mentally and physically, than their opponents.

Saracens had suffered huge body blows as they sampled the other side of a scrap for silverware in Cardiff, feeling the agony of being edged out by a star-studded Toulon side in the Heineken Cup Final at the Millennium Stadium.

Saints watched that game, which took place the day after they beat Bath, closely as they formulated their plan to pile more misery on a Saracens side who had impressed in topping the Premiership's regular-season table.

'We try to take lessons out of how Clermont [Saracens beat them 46-6 in the Heineken Cup semi-final] and Toulon played against Saracens,' Mallinder said. 'Sarries are very, very good and even harder to beat once they get ahead. Clermont showed that when you go a few points behind and start to overplay against them you play into their hands.

'We want to start well. We won't go out with the intention of not starting well, but what we have shown is that belief and fitness levels and strength in the squad that we can play for the full 80 minutes. We've done that in the past few games now.

'You look at our 23 and we are strong. We could name a number of players who could start easily and some of those players will be coming off the bench and hopefully bringing us home.'

As the days ticked by and the final edged ever closer, the significance of it really started to be emphasised. Mallinder, for his part, talked about doing it for the Barwells. For Keith, Leon and the rest of the family. You could feel the emotion around Franklin's Gardens, as Mallinder said: 'Leon Barwell's had a massive influence on this club. A year or so ago when we seemed to be stalling a little bit, he was the one who came and pushed us on.

'He said "we've got to keep growing as a team and we can't let other clubs beat us, we've got to go with them".

'Leon was a massive influence in bringing players to the club. He was very, very keen on doing it and we talk about Leon a lot, in terms of our team and our motivation.'

If Saints had needed any extra motivation, there it was, in the director of rugby's words and in the actions of the former chairman. It almost felt like they were meant to win the title. That this was their time. However, Saracens would say differently, and all the predictions were for the most nail-biting of Premiership Finals between two clubs who had grown to know each other like feuding siblings.

It would be a game decided by fine margins, by which team's stars stepped up at the crucial moments and how the squad united when it mattered most.

There was no doubting what it would mean to everyone at Saints and every supporter of the club. There was no doubting just how big this occasion would be. As fans flocked to Twickenham for the second year in succession, they hoped that this would be the year they would witness the Premiership trophy being lifted by the men wearing their team's shirts.

Game 39: Saturday, 31 May 2014: Saracens 20 Northampton Saints 24 (Aviva Premiership Final)

Saracens: Goode; Ashton, Bosch, Barritt, Strettle (Wyles 57); Farrell (Hodgson 65), de Kock (Wigglesworth 51); Barrington (Gill 83), Brits, Stevens (Johnston 55), Borthwick (c), Botha (Hargreaves 51), Brown, Burger (Wray 51), B Vunipola.

Saints: Foden; K Pisi (Stephenson 90), G Pisi (Wilson 62), Burrell, North; Myler, Fotuali'i (Dickson 51); Corbisiero (A Waller 55), Haywood (Hartley 55), Ma'afu (Mercey 51), Manoa (Day 57), Lawes, Clark (Dowson 57), Wood (c), Dickinson.

Referee: JP Doyle

Attendance: 81,193

Tries: Saracens: Marcelo Bosch. **Saints:** Ben Foden, George Pisi, Alex Waller

Conversions: Saints: Stephen Myler (3)

Penalties: Saracens: Owen Farrell (3), Charlie Hodgson (2). **Saints:** Stephen Myler

---

This was for all of the seasons when supporters dared to dream. For all the years they told others that this was their team's time. For all the years when those prophecies didn't come true. This was for those routinely melancholy months of May. For the heartbreaking Heineken Cup Final defeat to Leinster in 2011. For last year's Premiership showpiece loss to Leicester.

This was for the tortuous play-off semi-final defeat at home to Saracens in 2010. For the excruciating play-off semi-final loss at Tigers in 2011. For the harrowing defeat at Harlequins in 2012.

This was for all those times when victory was just seconds away, yet snatched so cruelly from Saints' grasp. This was a season when the tables turned.

This was for the Barwell family. For Leon who would have been looking down with a smile etched on his face. The late chairman did so much to steer the ship out of choppy waters last season. This was for every question Leon answered and acted upon at the fans' forum in February last year. For all the hours he put in to bring the likes of George North and Alex Corbisiero to this town.

This was for Keith Barwell, the man who has poured money into the club's coffers since the early days of professionalism. This was for every time his commitment looked like it wouldn't be rewarded with the Premiership trophy it merited.

This was for young Luis Ghaut, who bravely battled his illness to ensure he would be able to walk out alongside his heroes at Twickenham. The inspirational mascot deserved a celebration. He got one.

Who else was this for? This was for all of those men who weren't able to play a part in the final. For Tom Collins, Ethan Waller, Ross McMillan and many, many more who helped put the club in position for a Premiership Final appearance.

This was for all those coaches who have worked so intently to bring players through the Saints system. For all those who have ensured the potential of players like Courtney Lawes and Alex Waller, whose last-gasp try won the title for his home town club, was realised.

This was for Jim Mallinder. For Dorian West. Two men who have been steadily building to this deafening crescendo since arriving at Franklin's Gardens in 2007.

The gamut of emotion on their faces told the tale. The hours they have put in to restore their club among the elite deserved this. This was for them.

And this was, of course, for all of those who have supported this club through thick and thin. For everyone who helped pack out the Gardens even when their side was relegated to England's second tier.

This was for those who don the green, black and gold (or lime) and travel mile after mile to drive their team on in the toughest of away games. For those who were at Exeter, at Newcastle and many other stops on the route to Premiership glory.

This was for every time these players have been labelled bridesmaids. For every time the likes of Leicester and Saracens have celebrated, while Saints took a seat in the shadows.

This day at Twickenham, this 100 minutes of intense, bone-crunching rugby, was worth it, because Saints brought home the trophy. No more are they the nearly men. They are the main men. They are the champions of England.

Mallinder stood with a huge smile on his face and mouthed the word 'yes' twice as he desperately hoped that this was his team's time. He had seen his players celebrate what they thought was a try scored in the dying embers of extra-time by prop Alex Waller.

However, official confirmation would not come that soon. Instead, it was up to Television Match Official Graham Hughes to make the decision that would signpost the direction of the title. Hughes took his time, with every second feeling like an hour as he relentlessly replayed Waller's dart from a forward shove. Had the ball touched the line? Could Hughes really be clear that Saints had scored the try that would claim their first Premiership crown?

Tick, tock, tick, tock. Players, coaches and fans waited for the call that would change a club's history forever. Then they came, the six words that every Saints fan wanted to hear.

'JP, you may award the try.'

Those listening on ref link had a couple of seconds' head-start on everyone else and there were pockets of celebration, including, shamelessly, in the press box, where those connected to Northampton started to celebrate a monumental triumph.

Then the decision reached everyone as referee Doyle raised his arm to signal that Saints, yes Northampton Saints, were champions of England.

Myler still had the task of slotting the conversion to finish the game, which he did, and the party could then start on the Twickenham turf.

Players and coaches were united in delight as they struggled to find the right way to celebrate an incredible achievement. George Pisi led an on-pitch haka, while Corbisiero perhaps found the best way as he took his 'Yes, Yes, Yes' chant to the masses.

The England prop, a big wrestling fan, had taken it from Daniel Bryan and it had started to become commonplace at the Gardens. However, this was on a different scale as thousands of supporters chanted it in celebration with their popular front row forward.

Corbisiero would later perform a rap in the Saints dressing room and it was watched thousands of times after being uploaded to YouTube. They were great scenes and ones that would live long in the memory.

For Mallinder and his coaches, it was the culmination of seven years of hard work since starting life with Saints in the

Championship. The club had been lifted out of the second tier after one season and had steadily built to this moment.

All the semi-final and final agony faded as Mallinder performed media duties, in far happier circumstances than a year earlier, when that loss to Leicester hit everyone so hard.

'It's a real sense of relief to get over and win,' said Mallinder, who was to sign a new five-year deal at Saints two days later.

'We're pleased with last week's Amlin [Challenge Cup] win, but this week was always at the top of the agenda.

'It's fantastic for the club. It's a first Premiership title and particularly after coming close last year and in the Heineken Cup [in 2011], it's a special moment.

'It's the best. It's why you come to a big club like Northampton, to win trophies like this.

'We've been on the up in those seven years that I've been here. We've had some disappointments, but we've always talked after those about when we won a big one it would be sweeter. And it is.

'The experience of playing in big games is important. We're getting used to playing in big games.

'We've got senior internationals getting more games and international rugby, and we've got three great additions [Fotuali'i, North, Corbisiero] who have added to the mix.'

Those stars had helped Saints shake off their 'nearly men' tag, and how delighted everyone was with the first major trophy triumph since 2000.

Saracens threatened to spoil the party as they came back from 7-6 down at half-time and had the chance to win it as Charlie Hodgson lined up a conversion at 14-14. However, he hit the post to send the tie into extra-time, and after Hodgson slotted two penalties to Myler's one in the added period, Saints showed their fighting spirit, going through phase after phase before Waller burrowed his way to the line.

For players like Lee Dickson, who had walked through the Millennium Stadium mixed zone in tears after the Heineken Cup Final loss to Leinster three years earlier and also sampled the Premiership Final defeat to Leicester in 2013, glory had finally come after so much heartache.

'Last year was devastating,' Dickson said. 'We have got to finals before, we've got to the Heineken Cup Final, we've been to LV= finals, and we've just not won.

'We knew this time it would be all about little margins, and I think we played the game well. We controlled it well, and just got that edge we needed in the last minute.

'It was an amazing feeling. We have been on the other side of it, and it is nice to be on the winning side now.'

Those words would have been echoed a thousand times over, by supporters and players as they delighted in a season that was so special.

The double had been done and the title everyone really wanted had been won. As former chairman Keith Barwell said, it was the best season of them all. Now it was time for Saints to really step up the celebrations as they headed back to Franklin's Gardens for a party in the evening and a civic reception a day later.

The aftermath

SUPPORTERS had packed into the Rodber Suite to welcome their heroes back from Twickenham. With a constant ear being kept open for news of when the team bus would return, fans waited in excited anticipation.

They could not wait to see the men who had made the dream come true up close and pass on their individual congratulations to each and every one.

Finally, the black bus pulled into the car park at the front of the ground and fans flooded outside to get a glimpse of the players, coaches and, of course, the Premiership trophy.

The atmosphere was incredible as chants started to echo around and each player was given a rousing reception as they stepped off the bus.

Then came a moment to really savour as Mallinder, one of the last to get off, emerged with a grin the size of the Gardens pitch emblazoned on his face.

The chants began, 'Oh When The Saints' grew louder and louder, and, to everyone's delight, Mallinder, who may have had a beer or two on the way back, joined in with real gusto, soaking up every second of the adulation.

It was a fantastic connection between fans and director of rugby, the kind Leon Barwell had done so much to foster during his time at Saints.

Leon would have loved it. He would have relished seeing just how his hard work had panned out and how the club had reaped the rewards of his actions.

He wouldn't have taken too much credit for it, of course, because he was never one to bask in the limelight, but he would have had a feeling of real satisfaction. Thankfully, his children, Henry, Ben and Phoebe, were at the Gardens that night, enjoying the day and verbalising just how their father would have felt about this moment.

It was a moving conversation on an emotional day for those of a Northampton persuasion, and the celebrations were to continue long into the night as players headed off to town after spending plenty of time with their adoring fans.

In fact, so good was the night out, that a friend took a picture with Wilson and van Velze having given them a lift after seeing two men walking through the McDonald's drive-through with a big trophy.

The friend wasn't sure who they were initially, but he soon knew as he happily picked them up and posed for a selfie with them and the trophy as they brought the curtain down on a night of elation.

The players then had to pick themselves up the next morning, still hung-over, as they boarded a bus for the tour of the town, with the celebrations eventually finishing in a packed market square.

Thousands of supporters turned out to see the two trophies on show and to demonstrate what this team meant to the town.

A sea of Saints fans took over, with the players getting exactly the kind of response their season in the sun had merited.

Many were still drinking, topping up from the night before as what had happened during the past few weeks continued to sink in.

Players would be heading off on tour just a day later, with Waller among the men called up by England for their trip to New Zealand to take on the All Blacks.

However, whatever happened there, it would not eclipse the events the players had been part of at their club during a year that would never be forgotten.

The reaction

SO just what did this incredible season and all that was achieved mean to the men involved?

'It was almost life-changing,' says Wood as he sits in the stands at the Gardens and reflects on the double-winning campaign. 'The [Premiership] final is something I will watch for the rest of my life and look back on over and over.

'Hopefully I'll be able to show my kids that when I'm 70 years old and I'll be an old glory-day guy talking about those things. It's just a great feeling to feel like you've contributed to the history of this club.

'There have been some amazing players here, but, actually, no one's ever done that before. No one's ever done what we did.

'For this group of lads to have achieved that was just an amazing moment in the club's history.

'It never quite hit home until we returned home for the bus tour and everything else with 30,000 fans.

'We actually pulled out of the stadium thinking, "This might be a bit much, you know, sitting at the top of a bus, drinking during the day and what if no one's there?"

'We pulled out of the Gardens thinking "it might be a bit of a flop, this". To turn up in the centre of town and there's 30,000 people in the market, having pictures on the steps, lads are doing their hakas and songs – it's just an amazing feeling.'

Wood had been the man who kick-started a crazy three weeks at the end of that magical month of May as he scored the try that downed Tigers at the Gardens.

'It still feels like a bit of a blur to be honest,' he said.

'It was an amazing occasion and everyone's said that the atmosphere's never been better here.

'It was the way in which we won it, the way in which we were under massive pressure, we were down to 14 men and on any other day you could have fallen away.

'We just found it within ourselves to keep that belief, keep playing and to play to the death.

'Obviously scoring the try was massive but how often do you see a team score a try, take the points and then go back into their own half and drop the ball from the kick-off, there's a knock-on or a penalty and they kick for the win.

'The crucial thing for me was the composure to receive the ball, play a couple of phases and then get the ball off the pitch nice and calm. That could have gone wrong ten times over.'

So could the final, with Saracens threatening to win it, but paying the price for a missed kick from Charlie Hodgson and their failure to finish Saints off.

Instead, it was the character and never-say-die spirit of the Northampton players that shone through.

'It was such an emotional day,' Wood said. 'There had been so many near misses and what-ifs over the past few years where we'd been so close to achieving and not quite got there.

'It felt like it could have slipped through our fingers with the way the game had gone.

'I'd been a big driver in terms of talking about fitness and how they didn't have the front row replacements they were used to having. They were going to ask their props to go the distance and we'd spoken all week about how fitness was going to be key and how we had to keep believing no matter what the scoreline.

'We felt we could beat them and for that to come true was just an amazing feeling and that spurred us on to go on to the Challenge Cup Final and Premiership Final and get the results we needed there.

'That became our template as far as we did similar to Bath, who came out of the blocks, had a great start and had some of their key players playing really well in the first half. But we kept believing and kept talking about fitness and finishing strong and we beat them well in the second half as well.'

Saints could easily have felt their work was done after beating Bath to win the Challenge Cup, but they kept their determination levels high and hit their straps at exactly the right time.

'To be able to peak at the right time, to catch teams unaware and just know you're on the home straight – there's something to be said for that,' Wood said.

'We just nailed that that year. It just felt like it was our time and we felt like we were fitter and stronger than everyone else at the right time of year.

'Other teams had played really well, but we just felt that with the squad we had that it was our moment.'

It certainly was, and the man that made sure of that was final hero Waller.

He also delights in remembering the 2013/14 season, with an indelible smile etched on his face as he looks back on it.

'It was great for me because we had Corbs, but he was unfortunate with injuries and it was sort of my breakthrough year,' Waller said. 'It was one of my biggest seasons to prove myself as a starter and I loved every minute of it.

'It all merged into one, but we had team spirit bringing everything together and Phil [Dowson] led that brilliantly along with Dyls [Hartley] and Woody. That year was a brilliant year and to win the Premiership and the Amlin together was fantastic. I was lucky enough to go on tour with England as well and there were a lot of personal highlights, but the big one has to be winning the Premiership with the boys.

'Everyone will mention that try at the end when it comes to me, but we wouldn't have got there if the lads hadn't worked as hard and put their bodies on the line. For me, we did it as a team that year and all the boys who have come and gone will still have that feeling, which is a massive thing.'

So as he mentioned it, what about that try that won the final and, ultimately, the club's first Premiership title?

'My nose was bust, I had four or five stitches in my face and I've got Courtney [Lawes] to thank for that because it was his head that hit me as we tackled Jackson Wray at the same time,' Waller says, grinning.

'I was battered and bruised but I was just over the moon and you can't really put into words how it feels. Obviously all the fans were elated and that was brilliant. You've just won this trophy and it's what you've been trying to do for so many years.

'I'd come through the Academy and I'd seen the lows and the highs. I was involved in the final the year before and I'd seen semi-final defeats, having been involved in a lot of those.

'It meant a lot to all of the boys, especially the senior lads who had been involved from the start and it was just great.

'I just remember Tom Mercey coming up to me after the game and rubbing my face forgetting that I had six stitches in it and a broken nose, so I appreciated that!

'I poured Champagne over my head and then realised it really stings when it goes in cuts, but it was a great couple of weeks and it's all a bit of a blur and a haze because I had too many shandies.'

While Wood was the hero against Leicester and Waller took up the mantle against Saracens, one man who shone in every knock-out game was Myler.

Man of the match in both finals, the kicking king who had joined Saints from rugby league side Salford City Reds in 2006 had enjoyed the season of his life.

'It was a funny season,' he says, initially struggling to find the words to sum it up. 'We were involved in quite a few tight games but somehow we just kept finding a way to win, and that's what you need in big games.

'There's not a lot to separate the top teams and it often comes down to who reacts quicker or a slight decision here or there and we seemed to be on the right side of a lot of close games.

'It is really hard to win games back to back, particularly high quality games with a lot riding on them.

'The big thing for us was that when we were in those tight games, there was a belief in that squad that we were going to win, it didn't matter how long it took. We proved that in the final because it was the last minute of extra-time and we still believed we were going to do it.

'Looking back on it, it was very successful from an individual point of view, but I try not to think of it individually. Those kind of things just happen, but it was about the squad and sharing it with friends that I've played with for years was an unbelievable feeling.'

So just how did it feel to be the team that won that first Premiership title for the club?

'It makes you feel proud,' Myler said. 'We'd come close before, we'd struggled, been there or thereabouts and not quite made it, but we didn't want to give in.

'We still had ambitions of reaching that height again and we're obviously very proud because to be that team to win that first domestic title was an incredible achievement for the players and one that can never be taken away from us.'

Myler was involved in so many key moments during the campaign, winning games late with his ice cool kicking.

However, the matches that really stood out, understandably, were the ones in May.

'There were a lot, I played a lot of games and thinking towards the end of the year, the most memorable games were the semi-final and final,' he said.

'There were huge moments when Woody scored in the corner against Leicester and Alex sneaked over the line against Saracens in the final.

'At the end of the final, people were running on the field, absolute carnage was going on and the referee was telling me that I had to kick the conversion and I'd already booted it into the crowd. I had to finish the game before I could start celebrating.

'It was a crazy three weeks with the Amlin Cup the week before and we wanted to celebrate that but we couldn't because we knew we had a bigger prize to aim for the week after.

'It was an unbelievable period.'

So that was what it meant to some of the men involved in inspiring Saints on the pitch, but there was a young boy who certainly inspired them off it.

Luis Ghaut, a huge Saints fan, had almost become an extra member of the squad during the second half of the season. The 13-year-old had been diagnosed with osteosarcoma, a rare bone cancer, at the age of 11, but he battled bravely, attending several games at the Gardens while receiving treatment.

He found the strength to be the mascot at the Premiership Final and posed with Corbisiero and Wood, the two players who had spent the most time with him, after the final whistle.

Luis was a hero to his heroes and Wood even dedicated the play-off semi-final win against Leicester to him, insisting his bravery was one of the key motivating factors for the stirring success. Luis had helped to create great memories at Saints and he had plenty of his own as the team did him proud in achieving the double. The youngster and club were a partnership that had the greatest effect on each other.

Sadly, the Old Scouts full back was to pass away in September, 2014 and the Saints players wore t-shirts emblazoned with 'Hero to his Heroes' as they warmed up for a Premiership game against Bath in the season after the title triumph.

That was how much he meant to them and to the club, with his memory continuing to live on in the form of the Luis Ghaut Saintsman award, which is now given out to a young player whose commitment to their team's cause, positive attitude and fair play has stood out during that day's particular tournament.

Having written a tribute to Leon Barwell before the title-winning season, I wrote another, to Luis, ahead of the meeting with Bath during the early stages of the 2014/15 campaign.

When Saints run out at Franklin's Gardens on Saturday, they will do so with sadness in their hearts and motivation in their minds.

On Tuesday, the squad lost one of its members. He may not have been a player, but the part he played in last season's success was no less substantial.

Luis Ghaut, who lost his battle with osteosarcoma, was a 13-year-old with a broad smile and an infectious attitude which spurred Saints on last season.

When Saints beat Leicester in the magical Aviva Premiership semi-final back in May, Tom Wood, who scored the crucial try, dedicated the win to Luis.

It was a post-match interview that could have been used to extol the virtues of beating the old enemy or to bask in the glory of grabbing that memorable score.

But Wood had no time for that.

He wanted to talk about the 'incredibly inspiring lad' who had driven Saints over the line.

And it was more of the same on Premiership Final day two weeks later.

Luis had undergone major surgery in the weeks leading up to the Twickenham encounter with Saracens, but he battled to be ready to fulfil his role as the club's mascot.

And his presence was inspiration enough to help drive Saints to their first league title at the expense of Saracens.

Alex Waller's try in the final play of extra-time won it.

Saints had kept fighting until the end – just as Luis did.

Put simply, there are not many teenagers who can claim to be a hero for their heroes. Luis was.

'He's been phenomenal,' said Saints scrum half Lee Dickson. 'For someone at such a young age to have something like that is terrible but the way he acted and the way his family acted was just a credit to them.

'He was always here with a smile on his face and whatever was happening, he always wanted to be with the boys.

'He was the bravest little kid around, no doubt about it. He was a brave little soul. He's an inspiration for us.'

This Saturday, when Bath come calling in Northampton, he will not be there in person, but his spirit will remain.

And you wouldn't fancy being in the away camp with such a fired-up home side lying in wait.

Wood and Co will know the events of this week are about more than rugby.

But they will also know they have a job to do – and will, once again, call on Luis for inspiration.

And with thoughts of him reverberating around the Gardens this weekend, they have all the motivation they need to do one of their biggest fans proud once again.

Saints did go on to beat Bath, winning an enthralling Gardens encounter 31-24.

Luis would have been looking down cheering, but his real glory had come the season before, as it had for everyone of a Northampton persuasion.

Saints would go on to finish top of the Premiership regular-season standings for the first time in the club's history in the 2014/15 season, but they were unable to claim the silverware.

It wasn't their year. It wasn't to be a repeat of the season before. But then again, what could be?

A season bookended by the loss of key members of the Saints number had mixed grief with glee and no matter what had happened before and what would go after, no one at Franklin's Gardens would forget that year.

It was a once in a lifetime experience. An experience that meant so much to so many.

It was the season when Saints went from regular end-of-season sinners to Premiership and Challenge Cup winners.

It was the year of the Saint.